RORKE'S DRIFT
and
ISANDLWANA

RORKE'S DRIFT
and
ISANDLWANA

22nd January 1879:
MINUTE BY MINUTE

Chris Peers

Greenhill Books

Rorke's Drift and Isandlwana

First published in hardback in 2021
by Greenhill Books, Lionel Leventhal Ltd

This paperback edition published in 2021 by
Greenhill Books,
c/o Pen & Sword Books Ltd,
47 Church Street, Barnsley,
S. Yorkshire, S70 2AS

www.greenhillbooks.com
contact@greenhillbooks.com

ISBN: 978–1–78438–756–3

CIP data records for this title are available from the British Library

Designed and typeset by Donald Sommerville
Maps by Peter Wilkinson

Printed and bound by CPI Group (UK) Ltd,
Croydon CR0 4YY

Typeset in 12/15.5 pt Garamond Premier Pro Medium

Contents

———

Maps

Illustrations

Illustrations in Text

(All photographs © Chris Peers.)

Acknowledgements

———◆———

I would especially like to thank the following:

Michael Leventhal at Greenhill Books for his encouragement and patience while this book was struggling towards completion under rather difficult circumstances.

Professor John Laband for his extremely helpful advice and comments.

Paul and Christine Lamberth and the staff at Rorke's Drift Lodge, my hosts during my visit in 2015, for their unstinting help and hospitality.

Ray Boyles, who has put me in touch with numerous sources and contacts I might otherwise have missed.

And of course my family, Kate, Megan and John.

Chris Peers

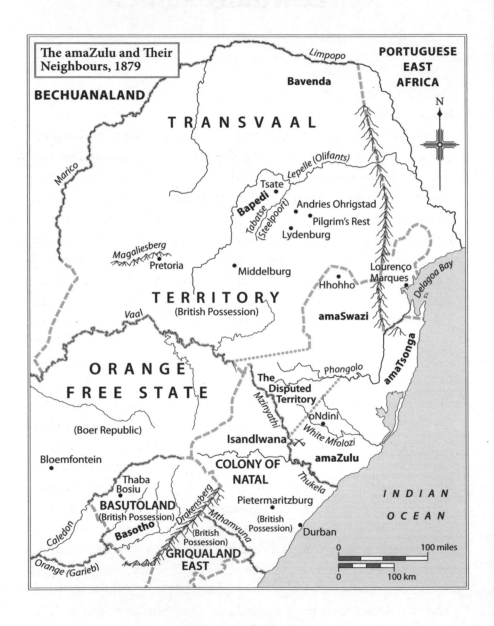

The amaZulu and Their
Neighbours, 1879

PORTUGUESE
EAST
AFRICA

BECHUANALAND

Bavenda

Limpopo

T R A N S V A A L

N

Marico

Lepelle (Olifants)

Tsate

Bapedi

Andries Ohrigstad

Tabatse
(Steelpoort)

Pilgrim's Rest

Lydenburg

Magaliesberg

Lourenço
Marques

Delagoa Bay

Pretoria

Middelburg

Hhohho

T E R R I T O R Y
(British Possession)

amaSwazi

Vaal

amaTsonga

O R A N G E
F R E E   S T A T E

Phongolo

The
Disputed
Territory

oNdini

(Boer Republic)

Mzinyathi

White Mfolozi

Isandlwana

Bloemfontein

amaZulu

COLONY OF
NATAL

Thaba
Bosiu

Thukela

BASUTOLAND
(British Possession)

Pietermaritzburg

Basotho

Drakensberg

(British
Possession)

INDIAN

OCEAN

Mthamvuna

Caledon

(British
Possession)

Durban

0   100 miles

Orange (Garieb)

GRIQUALAND
EAST

0   100 km

Introduction

Nearly a century and a half ago, in what was then an out of the way corner of southern Africa, a column of British troops set out to invade a local kingdom and put its ruler in his place. There was nothing particularly unusual in this; King Tewodros of Ethiopia in 1868, and six years later the Asante of West Africa, were only the most prominent among those who had already fallen to the superior military technology which the British armies could deploy. In the popular mind a contest between Africans and Europeans came down to a question of spears versus breech-loading rifles and artillery, and the outcome was entirely predictable. Yet, a few weeks after this invasion, on 1 March 1879, a cartoon appeared in the London satirical magazine *Punch*, entitled 'A Lesson'. It showed a chastened John Bull, representing Great Britain, sitting on a stool and watching an African warrior – a Zulu in his full regalia – writing on a blackboard the words 'Despise not your enemy'.

On 11 February, exactly a month after the troops had crossed the border, a telegram had arrived in London from their commanding officer, Lord Chelmsford, beginning with the words 'I regret to have to report a very disastrous engagement', and ending with a plea for urgent reinforcements.[1] The disaster was the destruction of most of the 1st Battalion, 24th Regiment of Foot, along with about a thousand supporting troops and local auxiliaries, by the Zulus at a place called Isandlwana. But along with that report also came what Chelmsford had hopefully called a 'little gleam of sunshine': the successful defence of the defeated army's supply base at Rorke's Drift by a single company of the 2nd Battalion of the 24th, against another Zulu force which had outnumbered them by around thirty to one. Incredibly, both the triumph and the disaster took place on the same day, 22 January 1879.

It is not surprising that both have earned their place among the most famous deeds in military history, and the details have been argued over and dissected in the minutest detail ever since. It is to be hoped, nevertheless, that the approach adopted here still has something new to offer. Rather than recounting the battles at Isandlwana and Rorke's Drift as two separate stories, or following the adventures of individual participants in turn, the events of this momentous day will be treated as a single minute-by-minute narrative.

This campaign is a complex subject for this sort of treatment, and not only because of the number of separate forces moving and interacting within a small area. All battles are traumatic events, but Isandlwana and Rorke's Drift were exceptionally so for the participants on both sides. The Zulus had never before encountered anything like the volume and accuracy of the British rifle fire, and their losses were extremely high both in victory and defeat, while surviving British soldiers either witnessed the wholesale massacre of their comrades or, at Rorke's Drift, were forced to fight for their lives at very close quarters for up to five hours without a break. Consequently most of the accounts of the fighting which we have come from men who had experienced tremendous psychological stress – a factor which was not often acknowledged at the time, and which they certainly would have been reluctant to acknowledge themselves. Almost every survivor must have suffered from some sort of psychological trauma, so it is not surprising that their recollections are often patchy or inconsistent. This is especially the case with regard to timings, and even the exact sequence of events was recollected differently by different people. There are a few surviving orders or dispatches from the British side which carry a note of the time they were issued, and these can occasionally be used to anchor the narrative, but even in these cases human error is always a possibility. So it is often impossible to be absolutely certain when particular events took place, or even sometimes the order in which they did so. Instead it is necessary to decide between differing accounts based on their inherent plausibility. In particular we need to bear in mind the difficulty of traversing the often steep and rocky terrain, and allow a realistic amount of time for the participants to cover the ground between successive positions. So, while I believe that the reconstruction offered here is as plausible as the evidence permits, all timings must nevertheless still be regarded as approximate.

Another issue to be borne in mind is the inevitable imbalance between the British and Zulu sources. We do have the recollections of a few of the Zulu participants, largely thanks to the oral historical material collected after the war,[2] but the Zulus were not a literate society at this time, whereas there is a large number of written accounts from survivors of all ranks on the British side. The result is that we do not know for certain, for example, whether the manoeuvres of the Zulu army before the battle were part of a preconceived plan to deceive Lord Chelmsford, or whether the course of events was dictated mainly by chance. All this uncertainty might be a problem from a scholarly point of view, but no one on that day, even the senior commanders, can have had much sense of being in control; all were reacting continually to unexpected crises which arose with bewildering suddenness, and none had any idea whether they would be on the winning side, or even live to tell the tale. If the narrative sometimes conveys this atmosphere of confusion, it has the advantage of reflecting what the experiences of the participants must have been like.

Note on Names and Terminology

Strictly speaking the name amaZulu, from which the English term Zulu derives, referred only to the original clan of that name which had formed the power base of King Shaka kaSenzangakhona (see pages 2–3), and to the royal house descended from him. In the nineteenth century the other groups which had been incorporated into the kingdom were identified by their own clan names.[3] However, outsiders, including the British, generally described all the subjects of the monarchy as Zulus, in the same way as we might speak of 'the Tudors' in English history, and this usage has been adopted here.

Where possible – except when quoting British sources directly – the names of geographical features have been given in the form used by the inhabitants of the country, the Zulus themselves. This is standard practice today, but it was not so in the nineteenth century, when Europeans routinely either used translated versions of the local names or made up entirely new ones. Thus for example the Mzinyathi River was referred to in British sources as the Buffalo ('*inyathi*' in the isiZulu language), but the hill known to the Zulus as Shiyane (or 'The Eyebrow') became the Oskarberg (named by the Swedish missionary Otto Witt in honour of his king, Oskar II). When the original name was retained, for example in the case of the hill called Isandlwana (perhaps because its meaning was obscure), it could appear in a wide variety of spellings, including for example Isandhlwana, Isandula and Insalwana. The generally accepted modern spelling, giving due regard to the role of prefixes in isiZulu (as the language of the Zulu people is known), is iSandlwana, but the Zulu language was not a written one in the 1870s, and so there is no definitively correct version. In these cases I have generally adopted the version most likely to be familiar to the English-speaking reader. Note that the location of King Cetshwayo's homestead is rendered here in its isiZulu form as oNdini, but the battle fought nearby in July 1879 is better known in its English version, Ulundi.

The British Army of the period measured distances in the old imperial system, and in the interest of reproducing as far as possible the original voice of the sources, the yards and miles quoted there have been retained here. Readers will not go far wrong if they regard a yard as roughly equal to a metre, and a mile as 1.6 kilometres.

Dramatis Personae

The following characters are central to the narrative, either because of the importance of their roles in the action, or because their recollections are particularly useful sources. Some brief introductory remarks may therefore be helpful.[4]

Frederic Augustus Thesiger, 2nd Baron Chelmsford, was the son of Frederic Thesiger, a lawyer who had been created Baron Chelmsford for his services as Lord Chancellor. The younger Frederic was educated at Eton, joined the Rifle Brigade at the age of eighteen, and later purchased a commission in the Grenadier Guards. He served in the Crimean War of 1855–6, in the Indian Mutiny in 1857, and in the Abyssinian Expedition of 1868, eventually returning to Britain as a colonel. He was a personal friend of the South African High Commissioner, Sir Henry Bartle Frere, whom he had known in India, and when he requested another overseas posting he was appointed to command the British forces in South Africa in 1878, with the rank of lieutenant-general. He campaigned successfully against the Xhosa in the Ninth Cape Frontier War, which ended in July 1878. In October he succeeded to the title of Baron Chelmsford after the death of his father. At the time of the Battle of Isandlwana he was fifty-one years old.

Anthony Durnford was born in Ireland in 1830. His family had a strong military tradition, and in 1848 he followed his father, General Edward Durnford, into the Royal Engineers. He was posted to various stations throughout the empire, but when he arrived in South Africa in 1872 he had never experienced combat. Nevertheless he was promoted to lieutenant-colonel in the following year. He was sympathetic towards black Africans and became friendly with the family of John Colenso, the Anglican Bishop of Natal, who was an active campaigner for their rights. In November 1873 he was tasked with leading a mounted force of Natal Carbineers and Basutos to intercept the amaHlubi led by their chief Langalibalele, who were attempting to flee towards Basutoland following a botched attempt to disarm them. His command got lost in the Drakensberg Mountains and arrived at their objective, Bushman's Pass, too late to block it. Durnford then attempted to negotiate with the amaHlubi, following his orders which were not to shoot first, but when firing broke out by accident his men dissolved into rout. Durnford was wounded in the arm, and despite his own personal courage and his adherence to his orders, he received most of the blame for the defeat. The Natal colonists were especially bitter against him because of his attempts (even though fundamentally justified) to blame the rout on the indiscipline of the Carbineers. Nevertheless, as the senior Royal Engineer officer in South Africa he served on the Boundary Commission of 1878, and before the war of 1879 broke out he was placed in charge of the raising and organisation of the local auxiliaries which would become the Natal Native Contingent, or NNC.

Richard Glyn was born in India in 1831, served in the Crimean War and the Indian Mutiny, and purchased the lieutenant-colonelcy of the 1st Battalion of the 24th Foot in 1867, being promoted to full colonel five years later. He and his battalion had been in South Africa since November 1875, and had fought with distinction in the Ninth Cape Frontier War of 1878, for which he was made a Companion of the Bath. Although a competent professional soldier, his main interest ('monomania' according to his orderly Nevill Coghill) was hunting – the preferred victim in South Africa, in the absence of foxes, being the black-backed jackal. When the invasion of Zululand began he was in command of Number Three Column, but Lord Chelmsford's decision to accompany this formation and control its day-to-day operations in person deprived Glyn of any useful role.

Henry Pulleine was born in 1838, graduated from Sandhurst and joined the 24th Foot as a lieutenant in 1858. He gained a reputation as an administrator and by 1877 was a brevet lieutenant-colonel, but had until then seen no actual combat. He served in the Ninth Cape Frontier War of 1878, then took over command of the army's main remount depot at Pietermaritzburg. In January 1879 he rejoined the 1st Battalion of the 24th in Zululand, and was placed in temporary command of the battalion when Colonel Glyn was put in charge of Number Three Column.

John Rouse Merriott Chard was thirty-one years old in January 1879. He had studied at the Royal Military Academy in Woolwich and received his commission as a lieutenant in the Royal Engineers in 1868. He had enjoyed an unspectacular but successful career so far, having been involved in the construction of fortifications in Bermuda and

Malta. In December 1878 he was sent to South Africa, and was placed in charge of the crossing of the Mzinyathi River at Rorke's Drift. His post-battle reports to Lord Chelmsford, and personally to Queen Victoria, are both reproduced as an appendix to Adrian Greaves's *Rorke's Drift*.

Gonville Bromhead was a couple of years older than Chard and had served in the 24th Foot since 1867, being promoted to lieutenant in 1871. He fought with B Company of the 2nd Battalion in the Ninth Cape Frontier War, and had taken over command of the company when his commanding officer was wounded by friendly fire.

Cetshwayo kaMpande was born around 1826. His parents were King Mpande kaSenzangakhona, who ruled Zululand from 1840 until 1872, and his queen Ngqumbazi. He was therefore a nephew of Shaka, the founder of the Zulu kingdom. In 1856 Cetshwayo won a brutal power struggle against his brother Mbuyazi. After this he remained the power behind the throne until he was proclaimed king in his own right in 1873, following his father's death. Although his accession had originally been supported by the British he pursued an increasingly independent foreign policy, strengthening his army, expelling the Christian missionaries whom he thought were threatening traditional Zulu culture, and resisting attempts by the Boers of the neighbouring Transvaal to annex his lands.

Dabulamanzi kaMpande was another of the sons of King Mpande, and thus a half-brother of Cetshwayo. He was around forty years old in 1879 and well acquainted with the white traders in Natal, from whom he had learned to ride and shoot. He held no official command position in the army, perhaps because the king regarded him as too impulsive, but he found himself by default the senior officer with the reserve corps at Isandlwana, purely on account of his royal blood.

Ntshingwayo kaMahole was probably around seventy years old in 1879, and thus a generation older than Cetshwayo. His father, Mahole, had been a close companion of Shaka's father, Senzangakhona. Ntshingwayo himself had fought in King Dingane's armies against the Boers in the

1830s, and in 1873 he was appointed to Cetshwayo's royal council. He was therefore one of the most important men in the kingdom and was famous for his oratory and his diplomatic skills, but he is not known to have commanded an army in battle before the Isandlwana campaign. In fact he shared the command with **Mavumengwana kaNdlela**, a younger officer who had been a friend of the king since their days as warriors in the uThulwana Regiment of the Zulu army. Mavumengwana's father had led the Zulus at the Battle of Ncome (or Blood River) in 1838, but his defeat there at the hands of the Boers seems not to have diminished the family's military reputation.

Another of the high-ranking Zulus at Isandlwana was **Zibhebhu kaMaphitha**, commander of the uDloko Regiment. Zibhebhu was '*inkosi*' or chief of a branch of the royal house, the Mandlakazi, and as such almost an independent ruler of his own fief in the north of the country. After the war he was to become Cetshwayo's deadly rival, but at the time of the Battle of Isandlwana he was still loyal, and was highly regarded for his military ability.

Mehlokazulu kaSihayo fought at Isandlwana as an *induna* (officer) in the iNgobamakhosi regiment. His command role was a junior one, and his significance in the story is due to two other factors. He played an important part in the events which precipitated the war, and in its aftermath he supplied his British interrogators with a very useful eyewitness account of the battle from the Zulu point of view.

Henry Curling was commissioned into the Royal Artillery in 1868, and in 1879 served, as a lieutenant, with N Battery of 5th Brigade. His letters relating to this campaign have been published in Greaves & Best, *The Curling Letters of the Zulu War*, described by Dr Greaves as 'the sole account from a front line survivor' of Isandlwana.

George Hamilton 'Maori' Browne, whose reminiscences were published in 1912 under the title *A Lost Legionary in South Africa*, is another very important source for events at Isandlwana. Browne was a notorious teller of tall stories and it is likely that this one is to some extent sensationalised, especially as far as re-created dialogue is concerned. However, it is at least certain that he was there (as he possibly was not in the Maori Wars in New Zealand from which he earned his nickname), and his account of Lord Chelmsford's state of mind at the time is of particular interest.

Frank Bourne joined the army in 1872 at the age of eighteen, and six years later was promoted to colour sergeant in B Company, 2nd Battalion, 24th Foot – the youngest NCO of his rank in the army at the time. He lived to be the last survivor of the defenders of Rorke's Drift, and his recollections are also published in Greaves, *Rorke's Drift*.

Prologue

1:30 a.m., 22 January 1879

'[In] our Cape affairs . . . every day brings forward a new blunder.' *(Benjamin Disraeli to Lady Bradford, September 1878)*

———

As he gets closer to his destination Lieutenant Walsh of the Imperial Mounted Infantry can discern faint white shapes ahead of him in the starlight, and he recognises the rows of canvas tents with a feeling of relief. Walsh has ridden ten miles through hostile country in the dead of night. In fact he has now made the journey twice, as he was sent out from the camp yesterday evening with rations and orders for the detached advance guard under Major Dartnell, and was unlucky enough to be selected to take Dartnell's report back to his commander-in-chief, Lord Chelmsford, on the grounds that he already knew the way.

It is chilly, very dark – tonight is the time of the new moon – and what looks in daylight like an open grassy plain is in fact littered with rocks and intersected by numerous steep sided ravines, or 'dongas', eroded by the frequent rainstorms.[1] Poisonous snakes, spiders and scorpions lurk in the long grass and in the crevices of the rocks, and there is always the possibility of running into warriors loyal to the king of the country, Cetshwayo kaMpande, who has vowed to defend it to the death. To the British even the stars of the southern hemisphere which provide Walsh with his only light appear alien.

The sentries at the camp at Isandlwana see the lone rider approaching and challenge him. Lieutenant Walsh gives the password and is allowed to enter. On either side of him the British soldiers in their tents lie in fitful sleep, exhausted after days of marching and labouring in the heat and humidity of a Zululand summer. So why are they here?

The Zulu kingdom lies not far inland from the endless beaches which fringe the Indian Ocean coast of what is now South Africa. In 1879 it had been in existence for about sixty years, and it had maintained relations with the British in the Cape Colony further south since 1824, when the kingdom's founder, Shaka, had first given permission for a group of white traders to reside there. The Zulus were a branch of the Nguni people, originally from further north, who by then had occupied the rich grazing lands of what is now KwaZulu-Natal Province for several centuries, but had never been united politically. In the late eighteenth century the people living north of the Thukela River and east of the Drakensberg Mountains were organised into four main clans, known as the Ngwame, Mthethwa, Ndwandwe and Qwabe.[2] Population pressure and the resultant shortage of grazing for their cattle gradually forced these groups into conflict with each other, but at first the slaughter was limited by traditional constraints on the waging of war. Battles consisted mainly of skirmishing and the hurling of spears and insults from a distance, a practice described by one informant as '*kisi* fighting', because the men would shout '*kisi!*' 'as if they were boys', as a warning to their opponents that they were about to throw a missile.[3] It was also considered contrary to custom to pursue and kill opponents who were running away. But about 1816 a young warrior named Shaka kaSenzangakhona (son of Senzangakhona), who had learned the art of war under the Mthethwa chief Dingiswayo, seized control of a small clan known as the amaZulu, or 'people of heaven', and reformed their army according to his own ideas. Throwing spears and skirmishing tactics were replaced by emphasis on killing at close quarters with the short stabbing spear or '*iklwa*', their users now protected by large cow-hide shields, which guarded most of the body and could even be used as weapons in their own right. The battle drill that the amaZulu were allegedly taught involved using the shield to hook an opponent's smaller shield and push it aside, at the same time spinning the victim round so that he could be stabbed under the right armpit.[4] As is usual with such drills, like those taught for twentieth-century bayonet combat, this probably seldom worked exactly as advertised, as a more lightly equipped enemy would soon become aware of the manoeuvre and do his best to avoid it. However, it would certainly have served to boost the Zulu's confidence and his willingness to seek decisive combat at close quarters. Europeans of the time often referred to the Zulu spears of both the throwing and stabbing types as 'assegais', although this is not a Zulu word. Also useful at close quarters was the heavy war club or '*induka*', known to the whites as a 'knobkerrie', which was carried even in peacetime and with which Zulu men practised fighting from an early age.

It is unlikely that these tactics were entirely new, and Shaka certainly did not invent the stabbing spear that came to be associated with them, but the impact of entire units fighting in this way was dramatic. Over the next decade Shaka's rivals were defeated one after another, and the survivors were either recruited into the Zulu army or forced to flee for their lives. The refugees took with them the lessons they had learned from Shaka and fell upon their more distant neighbours to the north and west in a violent upheaval that become known as the '*mfecane*', or 'crushing'. By the second half of the nineteenth century descendants of Shaka's Nguni victims were prominent among the Swazis to the north, the baSotho west of the Drakensberg, the Ndebele in what is now Zimbabwe, the Barotse of the Upper Zambezi and the Ngoni of Lake Malawi, while beyond them the Zulu-influenced Watuta roamed as far as the shores of Lake Victoria. The Zulu kingdom established by Shaka, however, remained the greatest military power of them all. Its founder was assassinated in 1828, but under his successors, his brothers Dingane and Mpande, it endured and prospered. The late 1830s saw bitter fighting against the Boers, farmers of Dutch descent, whose 'Great Trek' north from the Cape Colony began in 1836. In fact, Europeans had been in South Africa since long before Shaka. The Dutch had first settled at the Cape of Good Hope in 1652 and had been expanding northwards ever since. The British had occupied the Cape after the Napoleonic Wars, originally as a staging post on the route to India, and it was in an attempt to escape their domination that the Boers embarked on their Great Trek. In 1838, at the Battle of Ncome, known to the whites as

Blood River, Dingane's warriors attempted to attack a fortified Boer wagon *laager* and suffered a disastrous defeat. The discredited Dingane was subsequently overthrown by his half-brother Mpande, whose policy was to maintain peace with the encroaching white people. In 1844 the British in the Cape Colony annexed the land on the east coast south of the Thukela River, which early Portuguese navigators had named Natal, and although Shaka would have regarded this territory as part of his sphere of influence, Mpande did not oppose the move. Soon white settlers were pouring into Natal. There were sporadic clashes with the Zulus, but on the whole the latter's attention was focused more on their northern frontier with the rival Swazi kingdom.

In 1856 two of Mpande's sons, Mbuyazi and Cetshwayo, came to blows over the succession, culminating in a bloody battle at Ndondakusuka on the banks of the Thukela River in which Cetshwayo's faction, known as the uSuthu, massacred his brother's supporters, the isiGqoza. The survivors of the latter fled across the river and sought refuge in Natal, where they formed the nucleus of a growing community of Zulu dissidents, unhappy with the rule of Mpande and, after his accession in 1872, of Cetshwayo himself. Cetshwayo continued his father's policy of friendship with the settlers in Natal, regarding the Boers as a far more serious threat to his kingdom. In 1873 the king therefore invited the Natal Secretary for Native Affairs, Theophilus Shepstone, to take part in a coronation ceremony. However, this apparently friendly gesture was to lead to a great deal of trouble, because the two men saw its significance in very different ways. In Cetshwayo's opinion he was a legitimate monarch in his own right thanks to his descent from the royal house of Shaka, and it is highly unlikely that he intended the ceremony to signify that he sought the consent of the authorities in Natal to ascend the throne. Shepstone, on the other hand, saw fit to interpret events in just that way, and presented a list of new laws to which the king was said to have agreed as the price of British support.

At first Cetshwayo acquiesced, if reluctantly. For this was a dangerous time to be an independent black ruler in southern Africa. North of the Limpopo River most of the continent was still virtually unexplored by the white people, who did not begin to divide it up amongst themselves until after the Berlin Conference of 1884, but Zululand was in a very different position. Not only was it confronted by the settlers in Natal across the Thukela, but its western flank was threatened by the Boers, who had by now occupied the high plains of the Transvaal, just beyond the Drakensberg Mountains. The very existence of Natal was a destabilising factor in Zulu politics because of the ease with which dissident factions could find refuge there, and the lure of paid employment on white-owned farms which offered an alternative to military service at home for the young men. And the Boers, whose pastoral lifestyle required vast areas of land, were known to be casting covetous eyes on the Zulu pastures.

In the Cape Colony the British authorities, led by Sir Henry Bartle Frere, were pursuing a policy known as 'Confederation', which involved bringing all the territories south of the Limpopo into a formal alignment under their leadership.[5] The ultimate objective was still to guarantee the security of the vital sea route from Britain to India via the Cape of Good Hope, and in order to pre-empt any possible threat to the land borders of the Cape Colony it was considered necessary to disarm the remaining independent African powers in the region. Among these were the mountain kingdom of the Basotho (now Lesotho), the Pedi of what is now Limpopo Province of South Africa, the Korana who habitually raided the Cape from hideouts along the Orange River, Durnford's old enemies the amaHlubi, and the Xhosa, recently defeated in the Ninth Cape Frontier War. By the end of 1878 all of these groups except the Pedi had either been decisively beaten or forced into an uneasy subordinate relationship with the Colony; the Pedi, although their stronghold at Tsate did not fall until November 1879, presented only a local threat, of concern mainly to their neighbours, the Transvaal Boers. The Zulus, however, remained unsubdued, and their armies constituted not only a potential threat in themselves but an inspiration to their fellow Africans. Consequently, to many of the white population of Natal, the continued existence of a Zulu army was increasingly unacceptable. In 1877 British authority was established over the Boers in the Transvaal, and Theophilus Shepstone was sent to govern them. Whatever his previous sympathies may have been, he came to see it as his duty to support his new subjects in their territorial disputes with his former ally, Cetshwayo, and early in 1878 a Boundary Commission was set up to investigate the question of the border between the Transvaal and Zululand. Frere had hoped that the commission would support his contention that Cetshwayo was pursuing an aggressive expansionist policy and would need to be brought under control, but its report, produced in July, turned out to be strongly favourable to the Zulu claims.

This was a blow to Frere, who knew that Benjamin Disraeli's government in Britain was opposed to war with the Zulus, but believed that this would sooner or later be necessary in order to secure Natal and his planned Confederation. However, there were other pretexts which he could still make use of.

One of the catalysts for war was the action of a man who will feature prominently in the story of 22 January. In the summer of the previous year two of the wives of Sihayo kaXongo Ngobesi, the Zulu *'inkosi'* or regional chief based in the Batshe Valley, had eloped to Natal with their lovers. Sihayo's homestead was just across the Mzinyathi River from Natal near a place known as Rorke's Drift (a 'drift' being a ford or crossing place). Sihayo's son and heir Mehlokazulu kaSihayo had taken a party of several hundred warriors across the river there, and in separate incidents a few days apart they forcibly dragged the women away from the villages where they had taken refuge.[6] Sihayo was at the royal court at the time and was later able to deny any foreknowledge of the event, although the true extent of his involvement is not clear. The Natal bank was undisputed British territory, but the local border guards were not strong enough to intervene, and Mehlokazulu took the two women back to Zululand and executed them. This was the prescribed penalty for adultery among the Zulus, but it was not Mehlokazulu's responsibility to enforce it, especially since one of the women was his own mother. It was certainly contrary to British law, and the very fact that the Zulus could project their power so far without meeting any resistance made the settlers in Natal nervous. Sir Bartle Frere therefore sent a message to Cetshwayo demanding the extradition of Mehlokazulu and the other leading perpetrators. This was refused.

So when, in December 1878, a Zulu delegation attended a meeting with Theophilus Shepstone's brother, John, to discuss the findings of the Boundary Commission, they were presented with an astonishing ultimatum. Regardless of the justice of his territorial claims, Cetshwayo was now reminded of the 'promises' he had allegedly made at the time of his coronation, which were said to have included the abolition of the death penalty. He was ordered to surrender Mehlokazulu and Sihayo's other sons who had been involved in the incursion, to pay a fine of cattle as a penalty for not having done so sooner, to readmit the missionaries who had been expelled, and on top of that to disband his army. This latter demand was of course completely unacceptable for an independent ruler, and Frere and Shepstone knew it. It was undoubtedly intended to provide a pretext for a war, which with luck would be over long before the government in London knew it was happening.

The Zulu army that was so confidently written off had largely ceased its expansionist campaigns after Shaka's death, and had not fought a major war against the whites for more than thirty years. The trader Nathaniel Isaacs reported as early as the 1830s that it had lost much of its fighting spirit under Dingane. Nevertheless it was still – on paper at least – the most formidable fighting force in the region.[7] There was no standing army in the European sense, but Cetshwayo could call on as many as 40,000 trained soldiers, permanently enrolled members of the 'amabutho' or regiments established by Shaka and his successors. These 40,000 men represented what was probably the fourth-largest armed force south of the Sahara – after Ethiopia, Asante and Buganda – but among native African armies only the Ethiopians could compare with it in fighting power. Within its sphere of influence in southern Africa, therefore, the Zulu army was accustomed to almost unchallenged superiority.

As was the case in Nguni society generally, every male Zulu belonged to an age set, comprising men of the same generation, who would form the basis of a newly raised '*ibutho*' (the singular of *amabutho*) when they reached the age of about eighteen. Each such unit was established by the king, who then gave it a title and allocated it to a military village, or '*ikhanda*', of its own. (Nineteenth-century writers generally used the term 'kraal' for any African settlement, but this is not really appropriate, as a kraal is strictly speaking an enclosure for livestock. I am grateful to John Laband for reminding me of this.) After their initial training the youths then remained at the king's disposal for the next decade or so, until they were allowed to marry. In practice, however, they tended to be called up for a few months each year for training, campaigns or major ceremonies, and were allowed to return to their villages for the rest of the time.

Eventually they would be allowed to marry – though often not until they were in their thirties – after which they adopted the head ring, or '*isicoco*', which denoted their new status, and set up their own households. The married regiments were no longer summoned for routine military service, but they could be called up in emergencies, for example when their homeland was threatened. Although they might have lost a little of the fitness and enthusiasm of their youth, the married warriors were valued for their experience and their steadiness in battle. The events of 22 January 1879 were to show that they had lost none of their courage or their fighting skills.

Each regiment was subdivided into a number of '*amaviyo*', roughly equivalent to companies, although as recruitment to each *ibutho* was restricted to a particular age group neither they nor their constituent companies were of a standard size, but had to make do with the men available. The *amaviyo* were commanded by junior officers promoted from among the rank and file, but senior officers – usually three per regiment, two 'wing' commanders, left and right, and the officer in overall command – were appointed by the king. These men were known as '*izinduna*' (singular '*induna*'), and constituted what was in effect a professional officer corps. This helped to ensure that the warriors were trained and led in accordance with the tactical doctrine introduced by Shaka.

Discipline was strict, although less so than in Shaka's day, when whole units were allegedly executed for cowardice.

An '*impi*' (a term which could denote an independent force of any size) would inevitably attempt to employ the same basic fighting formation, which the Zulus, to whom cattle were a central part of their culture, described as the 'horns of the bull'. The centre, or 'chest', would advance to pin the enemy, while the youngest and fittest men would form the right and left 'horns' and spread out to envelop him from both flanks. Meanwhile the reserve or 'loins', usually composed of the oldest and most experienced warriors, remained in position behind the centre unless needed to reinforce their comrades or exploit a gap in the enemy's line. Once the enemy was surrounded the warriors would 'sweep everything clean' in hand-to-hand combat, leaving no survivors. Although defeated rivals might be recruited into the Zulu ranks after a successful campaign, during a battle and its immediate aftermath they traditionally took no prisoners. These envelopment tactics, and the ruthless pursuit of fugitives – both innovations introduced into Nguni warfare by Shaka – were to have a decisive influence on the course of the engagements at Isandlwana and Rorke's Drift.

A few senior officers rode horses acquired from the white men, but just as they had done in Shaka's day the typical Zulu marched and fought on foot, as did their commander Ntshingwayo, who intended to set an example to his men despite his advanced years. Nevertheless, a lightly equipped Zulu army could manoeuvre so rapidly that the Boers advised the British to take the same precautions as if they were facing cavalry. Each warrior was armed with an *iklwa*, an *induka* and a shield, although the shields tended to be smaller than in Shaka's day, and the stabbing spear was supplemented with a number of throwing weapons or '*isijula*', which had been banned by Shaka but reintroduced under Dingane. Each regiment had an elaborate 'parade uniform' consisting of feathered headdresses, cow tails and capes of animal fur, but if these outfits had ever been worn in battle this was no longer the case in 1879, when most men took the field in little more than a loincloth and, if married, a head ring. Shaka had also imposed a system of distinguishing shield colours for the *amabutho*, with each unit making its shields from the skins of cattle of a particular pattern or colour. Nguni cattle are still prized for the variety of coat colours which they display, but after the end of Shaka's wars of expansion the huge numbers of animals required to equip entire regiments with identical patterns were harder to come by, and by Cetshwayo's day the system had largely broken down. One basic principle still applied, however: white or mainly white shields were still reserved for senior regiments, while their newly raised compatriots had to make do with shades of black or brown.

Firearms had been introduced into Zululand by white traders during the reign of Mpande, and the most successful of these men, John Dunn, earned the favour of Cetshwayo by importing them on a large scale from the Portuguese in Mozambique. By the 1870s it is possible that as many as half of the warriors possessed a gun. Before the Isandlwana campaign Cetshwayo inspected his regiments and was disappointed by the scarcity of firearms, so he ordered every man who could afford to do so to go and buy one from Dunn, although the latter was trying unsuccessfully to remain neutral in the coming war. (He failed, and eventually became Lord Chelmsford's chief intelligence officer.) However, nearly all of the weapons that were acquired were obsolete muzzle-loading muskets discarded by European armies, whose range and rate of fire were far inferior to the Martini Henry rifles employed by the British. Furthermore few Zulus had the opportunity or the ammunition necessary to practise with their guns, so their aim was inevitably erratic and they tended to fire too high. Not surprisingly, they tended to incorporate firearms into their traditional tactics rather than trying to transform themselves into sharpshooters, simply firing a volley at close range before charging into contact in the same way as they employed their throwing spears.

Cetshwayo naturally rejected out of hand the idea of dismantling this army, and both sides made preparations for war. The king was anxious to present himself as the victim of unprovoked aggression, and so he gave no instructions to invade Natal; in fact he expressly ordered his commanders not to do so. But Lord Chelmsford, commanding the

British forces in South Africa, was instructed by Frere to make immediate plans to take the offensive. On 11 January 1879 the first troops crossed the border into Zululand. Five British columns had been assembled.[8] Number Five, under Colonel Hugh Rowlands, was deployed in a defensive role near the frontier with the Transvaal, while the others set out to converge on Cetshwayo's *ikhanda* at oNdini, which was about sixty miles from the frontier. Number One Column, led by Colonel Charles Pearson, crossed the Thukela River and advanced at the eastern end of the front, near the coast, aiming for the old mission station at Eshowe. Colonel Evelyn Wood's Number Four Column operated on the far left in the north-west, while Colonel Anthony Durnford's Number Two Column remained in reserve in the centre. The most powerful of the columns was Number Three, commanded by Colonel Richard Glyn of the 1st Battalion, 24th (2nd Warwickshire) Regiment of Foot, which crossed the Mzinyathi River in the centre of the line, at Rorke's Drift. The core of this column consisted of the two battalions of the 24th Foot. It was Glyn's misfortune that, as the main striking force, his column was to be accompanied by the overall commander, Lord Chelmsford. His presence meant that Glyn was sidelined and took little part in subsequent command decisions; he was still officially the column commander, but was now in effect part of Chelmsford's staff. His place at the head of the 1st Battalion was therefore taken by his less experienced subordinate, Lieutenant-Colonel Henry Pulleine. The 2nd Battalion was commanded by Lieutenant-Colonel Degacher. B Company of this battalion was left behind to protect the crossing at Rorke's Drift, under the command of Lieutenant Gonville Bromhead.

The men of the 24th were regular infantry, mostly veterans of the Ninth Cape Frontier War which had been fought against the Xhosa of the Eastern Cape the previous year, and armed with the British Army's most up-to-date weapon, the Martini Henry rifle. This was a single shot breech-loader, which still had to be loaded one round at a time like the older muskets, but its rate of fire was much faster and it was effective out to a much greater range – around 600 yards compared to 100 or less for the Zulu weapons. The powerful cartridge of the

Martini Henry also meant that it could inflict much greater damage on its target. It had its faults: the recoil was heavy, the barrel overheated after repeated firing, and as for every gun of the era its ammunition produced clouds of white powder smoke, which not only gave away a shooter's position but made it hard for him to acquire fresh targets once a few rounds had been fired.[9] Nevertheless, the British soldiers were confident that their weapons gave them a decisive advantage over any African opponents, a belief supported by their experiences in the Cape Frontier War, where Xhosa attacks had often been stopped at a range of 400 yards.[10] If the enemy did manage to get to close quarters the Martini Henry was also deadly in hand to hand fighting, thanks to the 22-inch bayonet or 'lunger' which, when fixed, converted the rifle into a thrusting weapon with a longer reach than the Zulu *iklwa*, and sufficient weight to penetrate the enemy's shields with ease.

Both the battalions of the 24th were divided into eight companies, designated A to H, each with a nominal strength of about 100 men, although casualties and sickness meant that they actually averaged around 70–80. Companies were commanded in theory by captains, though again in practice more junior officers, the lieutenants, often found themselves standing in. This was one of the last campaigns in which the British infantry fought in their traditional red jackets and dark blue trousers, though one concession to the climate was allowed in the form of a white cork sun helmet, which was generally camouflaged by staining the cover khaki. Each regiment was distinguished by the colour of the facings on the jacket – in the case of the 24th this was known as willow green.

Number Three Column's supporting artillery consisted of six 7-pounder horse-drawn guns from N Battery, 5th Brigade, led by Brevet Lieutenant-Colonel Arthur Harness. These guns were relatively light and short-ranged, but their mobility made them ideal for colonial campaigns in which the enemy was not expected to field anything of comparable firepower.

Glyn's force was also accompanied by a number of volunteer and irregular units raised in South Africa. The Natal Mounted Police provided about 130 men under Inspector Mansel. The remaining volunteers were organised into smaller mounted units of no more than 100 men each, raised from local white settlers and armed with a variety of breech-loading carbines, which were in effect lighter and slightly shorter-ranged versions of the Martini Henry rifle. They comprised the Natal Carbineers, Newcastle Mounted Rifles and Buffalo Border Guard, under the overall command of a former British regular, Major John Dartnell, who was well respected in frontier society. In fact the volunteers had flatly refused to serve under the officer originally selected for them, Lieutenant-Colonel Russell of the 9th Lancers, and had insisted upon Dartnell instead. Russell was transferred to lead the Imperial Mounted Infantry, regular soldiers who were mounted on horses for patrol and reconnaissance work, but not trained to fight as cavalry.

The column was also accompanied by a large number of African auxiliaries from the 2,000-strong 3rd Regiment of the Natal Native Contingent, or NNC, organised into two battalions and led by Commandant Rupert Lonsdale, a former officer in the Black Watch. One company of the 2nd Battalion under Captain William Stevenson was stationed at Rorke's Drift to support Bromhead's regular company. Most of the NNC men were of questionable military value, as they were poorly trained and equipped and were unenthusiastic about facing the dreaded Zulus. Only one man in ten was armed with a modern rifle, the rest having to rely on their traditional spears. This was at least partly because of the white settlers' fear that the NNC might one day use their weapons against them. Furthermore their (white) company officers and NCOs were of variable quality and often did not speak the men's language. An exception was the isiGqoza contingent, consisting of three companies. The isiGqoza were the descendants of the defeated Zulu faction who had escaped to Natal after the Battle of Ndondakusuka twenty-three years earlier, and were both well trained in Zulu fighting methods and determined enemies of Cetshwayo.[11]

At dawn on 11 January Lord Chelmsford led his column, both the fighting troops and their supply train of more than 300 ox-drawn wagons, across the Mzinyathi River at Rorke's Drift. It was the rainy season and the water was high, so the regular infantry were taken over on flat-bottomed, rope-operated ferries known as ponts, but the mounted men and the NNC had to wade across. To everyone's relief, there was no sign of the enemy.

On the following day Chelmsford and Glyn led a detachment to sweep the Batshe Valley, which runs towards the Mzinyathi from the north about two miles downstream of Rorke's Drift. Not only were the Zulu homesteads there a potential threat to his left flank as he turned east, but one of them was also the headquarters of Sihayo kaXongo, whose sons had been held responsible for starting the war.[12] Mehlokazulu was not there – he had already obeyed Cetshwayo's summons to join the royal army at oNdini – but his brother Mkhumbikazulu led the resistance, firing from a defensive position in dense scrub at the base of the cliffs which fringe the valley. The Zulus were eventually driven out by a frontal attack by the NNC, combined with an outflanking move by Chelmsford's mounted troops. Mkhumbikazulu and about thirty others were killed, and Sihayo's *ikhanda* was burned without further opposition. So far it did not look as if Zulu resistance was going to be particularly determined, but Chelmsford noted in his dispatches that he still hoped that Cetshwayo's main army would come forward and fight a pitched battle which would lead to their early defeat.[13] He need not have worried.

Cetshwayo quickly learned from his well-organised corps of messengers of the attack on Sihayo, and decided to fight holding actions against the other columns while he concentrated his strongest forces against the obvious main threat in the centre.[14] On 17 January his army began its march westward. Heavy rain and the need to bring up the slow-moving wagons delayed any further British advance for a few days, but on the 20th the column moved on again, leaving only the small detachment at Rorke's Drift to guard the crossing and the stores that had been left behind. This post consisted of what was – until it was commandeered by the army – the mission station of the Reverend Otto Witt of the Swedish Missionary Society. It was named after the man

The Batshe Valley seen from the Isandlwana road. The cliffs on the far side were the scene of Chelmsford's fight with Sihayo's men on 12 January.

who originally built it, Jim Rorke, a trader who had died a few years earlier, having reportedly shot himself when a consignment of gin failed to materialise. There were two rectangular thatched buildings: Rorke's house, now being used as a hospital, and Witt's former church, which had reverted to its original role as a storehouse. The military stores were looked after by Assistant Commissary Walter Dunne, a regular officer from the army's commissariat department. The hospital was the responsibility of Surgeon James Reynolds, the 1st/24th's regimental medical officer. In overall command was Brevet Major Henry Spalding, an officer belonging to Chelmsford's staff who had been placed in charge of the lines of communication between Helpmekaar, the main supply base on the ridge of the Biggarsberg Mountains ten miles to the west, and the front.[15]

The rest of the column's troops crossed the valley of the Manzimnyama River which ran across its route about three miles east of the Batshe, and established a new camp at the base of a prominent isolated mountain another mile further on, but still close enough to the river to ensure a good supply of water. This mountain was a very visible landmark for miles around, and reminded the men of the 24th Foot of a crouching lion or a sphinx, which coincidentally was their regimental cap badge, a battle honour won in Egypt in 1802. To the Zulus, with their strong relationship to their cattle, it resembled the second stomach of a cow. The local name for this feature, as the world was soon to learn, was Isandlwana.

The column's wagons were parked on a saddle, or 'nek' as it was known in South Africa, between Isandlwana and another hill, Mahlabamkhosi, a few hundred yards to the south. In front of them were the lines of tents, facing east across a plain which appeared to offer an unrestricted view as far as the Hlazakazi Ridge and a cluster of associated hills, Magogo, Phindo, Silutshana and Siphezi, around twelve miles away. Although Chelmsford did not know it, Cetshwayo's army was already in the vicinity, concentrated out of sight just behind Siphezi. On the southern side of the camp a steep rocky slope led down in the direction of a gorge through which the Mzinyathi River flowed south-eastward, while a mile away to the north was the escarpment of the Nqutu Plateau. This plateau was dead ground from the camp and so potentially a source of danger, but in fact lines of sight from Isandlwana were at least adequate in all directions except to the west, where the view was blocked by the hill. However, Chelmsford had no reason to expect any threat to emerge from that direction, and the camp was not expected to be occupied for more than a few days. It was common practice in South Africa to draw the wagons together into a *laager* to protect a military camp in case of a surprise attack, but this was not done at Isandlwana. The wagons were expected to be returning to Rorke's Drift shortly to bring up the rest of the supplies, and in any case, their commander considered, a force which included two battalions of British regulars was strong enough to protect itself without wasting time and energy on elaborate defensive arrangements.[16]

By the morning of 22 January, however, Number Three Column was no longer the strong united force that it was intended to be. Late on the 20th Chelmsford had ridden out to reconnoitre the Hlazakazi Ridge

The view east from the Tahelane Spur across the site of the British camp towards the Hlazakazi Ridge and the Mangeni Gorge, where Lord Chelmsford was chasing Zulus when the camp was attacked on 22 January. Isandlwana Hill and the site of the camp are just out of view to the right.

and realised that the broken country beyond, and especially the steep valley of the Mangeni river, would be an ideal location for the enemy to contest his advance. Particularly worrying was the presence of two local chiefs – both coincidentally named Matshana – whose allegiance was uncertain, but who were suspected of being in communication with Cetshwayo. So, early on the next day, Major Dartnell was ordered to make a reconnaissance in force, taking with him most of the column's mounted units and two battalions of the NNC.[17] They reached Hlazakazi late in the afternoon, but at first reported no sign of the enemy. In fact Cetshwayo's army was already several miles to the north, having marched behind the hills and up onto the Nqutu Plateau, where it had found a secure bivouac in and around a steep-sided ravine known as the Ngwebeni Gorge, some five miles north-east of where Number Three Column was camped.

Chapter 1

Before the Dawn, 22 January 1879

'We felt pretty certain that we would be attacked in the morning.' *(Henry Harford, with Dartnell's detachment)*

————◆◆◆————

12 midnight. Dartnell's men are bivouacked in the open, without tents, and are having an uncomfortable night. As darkness fell they could see camp fires burning in the distance and realised that the enemy was somewhere in front of them, unseen and in unknown strength. At some point – no one is quite sure what time it was – an NCO of one of the NNC battalions falls asleep, and wakes suddenly to see a dark shape approaching his position. It is in fact one of his own sentries, but instead of challenging the man the startled NCO fires a shot, which fortunately misses its target but provokes a panic in the camp.[1] Most of the NNC troops, believing that they are being attacked by the Zulus, flee into the night. Some semblance of order is eventually restored and the men driven back to their posts by their officers with harsh words and even blows from sticks. But no one expects to get much sleep after that – the men are still fearful of being attacked in the dark, even though night attacks are not a standard Zulu tactic, and the NNC officers dare not take their eyes off their men in case they run again. Lieutenant Walsh of the Mounted Infantry has already made the journey between the camp at Isandlwana and Dartnell's outpost once before in the dark to bring up rations, and now Dartnell asks him to return with a message for the commander-in-chief. The message advises Chelmsford that the Zulus facing him seem to be more numerous than anticipated, and requests reinforcements if he is to fight them in the morning.

1:30 a.m. Lieutenant Walsh reaches Isandlwana and reports to Major Francis Clery, Glyn's Adjutant-General, who wakes the colonel.[2] Glyn tells him to take the message straight to Lord Chelmsford, and Clery reads it to the commander-in-chief, lying on the ground next to his camp bed and peering at the crumpled paper by the light of a candle. Chelmsford is instantly wide awake, appreciating at once the significance of Dartnell's note. He has been worrying that the enemy will avoid battle, but now it seems that Dartnell has found their main body and, at least for the time being, fixed it in place. The general hurriedly gets out of bed and begins issuing his orders. He organises a column to march to Dartnell's assistance. As this force may have to engage Cetshwayo's whole army it needs to have sufficient strength for the job, so he allocates to it the entire 2nd Battalion of the 24th Foot, – less B Company, which is at Rorke's Drift, and Lieutenant Pope's G Company, which is on picket duty at the camp and cannot be relieved before morning. He also mobilises all the remaining mounted troops, and four guns from the artillery battery.

Then his thoughts turn to the post at Rorke's Drift, ten miles in the rear. Bromhead's company should by now have been reinforced by Colonel Anthony Durnford's Number Two Column, which has been ordered to move up there, but one company of regulars should be more than enough to defend the place. Chelmsford tells Clery to bring Durnford up to Isandlwana to act in his support. Chelmsford's senior staff officer, Lieutenant-Colonel John Crealock, can overhear the conversation from his neighbouring tent, and now he interrupts with a loaded question: 'Is Major Clery to issue orders to Colonel Durnford?'[3] The implication of mentioning their respective ranks in this way is that it is inappropriate for Clery to do so, because Durnford is not subject to Number Three Column but has an independent command. Chelmsford concedes the point, and asks Crealock to draft the order. This he proceeds to do, but in his haste he leaves the instructions ambiguous:

22nd, Wednesday, 2 am

You are to march to this camp at once with all the force you have with you of No. 2 Column.

Major Bengough's battalion is to move to Rorke's Drift as ordered yesterday. 2/24th, Artillery and mounted men with the General and Colonel Glyn move off at once to attack a Zulu force about 10 miles distant.

J.N.C. [John North Crealock]

If Bengough's battalion has crossed the River at Eland's Kraal it is to move up here.[4]

The reference to Bengough's battalion will remind Durnford unpleasantly of the way in which his command has already been eroded by interference from the commander-in-chief.[5] He was originally placed in command of an independent force based at Kranskop in Natal, which was intended to operate independently along the Mzinyathi River southeast of Chelmsford's own line of advance. His column consists of three battalions of NNC infantry, a battery of 9-pounder Hales rockets, and the African mounted troops who make up what is then known as the NNMC or Natal Native Mounted Contingent. This comprises three troops of Zikhali's horse, named after a former chief of the amaNgwane people from whom they have been recruited, one troop of Tlokoa, a branch of the baSotho, and one of men from the Edendale mission near Pietermaritzburg. These last are Christians, well-disciplined and well-disposed to the white settlers, and are led by Lieutenant Harry Davies. In overall commander is Lieutenant Alfred Henderson, who also leads the Tlokoa. The amaNgwane troops are under the command of Lieutenants Charlie Raw, Joseph Roberts and Wyatt Vause. The British, unable to distinguish between the various ethnic groups but aware of the reputation of the baSotho for horsemanship, tend to refer to them all as 'Basutos'. All the mounted troops are armed with breech-loading carbines. However, on 8 January, before the invasion has even started, Chelmsford has ordered Durnford to detach two of his NNC battalions to Sandspruit, which is about ten miles south of Helpmekaar

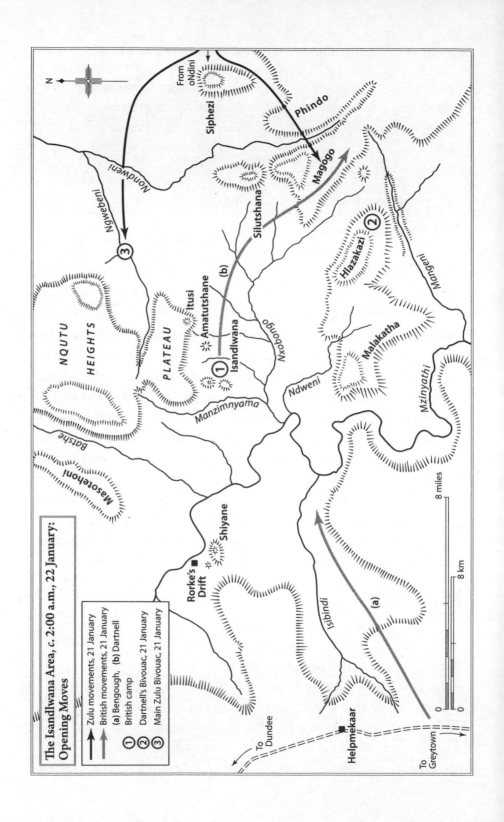

The Isandlwana Area, c. 2:00 a.m., 22 January:
Opening Moves

Zulu movements, 21 January
British movements, 21 January
(a) Bengough, (b) Dartnell
British camp
① Dartnell's Bivouac, 21 January
② Dartnell's Bivouac, 21 January
③ Main Zulu Bivouac, 21 January

N

NQUTU HEIGHTS

PLATEAU

Ngwebeni

Nondweni

From oNdini

Siphezi

Phindo

Magogo

Silutshane

Hlazakazi

Mangeni

Ntusi

Amatutshane

Isandlwana

Nxobongo

Malakatha

Ndweni

Mzinyathi

Manzimnyama

Masotsheni

Batshe

Shiyane

Rorke's Drift

Isibindi

Helpmekaar

To Dundee

To Greytown

8 miles

8 km

on the Greytown road. The rest of the column was told to wait on the Natal side of the river until further notice. Durnford objects and it is eventually agreed that only one battalion will be detached, the 2nd under Major Harcourt Bengough. Nevertheless, Durnford drags his heels, and several days later Chelmsford becomes aware that none of the units has moved.

What is worse Durnford has announced his intention to cross the river in response to a report that the Zulus are planning to launch a raid into Natal. Militarily this makes sense, but it provokes a written rebuke from Chelmsford, who brusquely threatens to sack his Number Two Column commander if he continues to ignore his orders. The C-in-C then issues a series of instructions regarding Bengough, who is first to remain at Sandspruit, then to march up to Rorke's Drift, and finally to cut across country to the river at the small settlement of Elands Kraal (a name which is usually rendered nowadays as a single word: Elandskraal). Unfortunately no one is sure which, if any, of these orders Bengough has received and is currently acting on. The result is that not only are Durnford and his commanding officer barely on speaking terms, but an entire battalion of the former's troops has effectively gone missing. If ever there is a moment when clear and comprehensive orders are necessary, this is it. A special service regular on the transport staff, Lieutenant Horace Smith-Dorrien of the 95th Regiment, is found to make the dangerous journey to Rorke's Drift in the dark. But the orders in his saddlebag are neither clear nor comprehensive.

3:30 a.m. Major Clery has spent the last two hours trying to muster the troops without any of the usual shouted commands or bugle calls, which he fears might alert a watching enemy. He has had to visit each company commander's tent individually to pass on the general's instructions, and by the time the men are starting to move Lord Chelmsford is dressed and impatient to be on the road. It suddenly occurs to Clery that Lieutenant-Colonel Pulleine, who will be the senior officer left in camp, has received no orders.[6] Chelmsford is too busy, and Colonel Glyn, as ever, would just refer him to the general, so Clery decides to issue the necessary orders in Glyn's name, but on his own initiative. As he is Glyn's chief staff officer he does not consider that he is exceeding his authority in the circumstances. He sends a note to Pulleine, then as an extra precaution he goes to the colonel's tent himself and repeats what he has written. The orders will not survive for posterity, but the major will later record what he remembers saying:

> You will be in command of the camp in the absence of Colonel Glyn. Draw in your line of defence while the force with the general is out of the camp. Draw in your infantry outpost line in conformity. Keep your cavalry vedettes still well to the front. Act strictly on the defensive. Keep a wagon loaded with ammunition ready to start at once, should the general's force be in need of it. Colonel Durnford has been ordered up from Rorke's Drift to reinforce the camp.

As far as the deployment of the outposts is concerned these instructions might be considered to be stating the obvious, but at least, in contrast to Crealock's note to Durnford, they are not ambiguous. Of course, as we have seen, Durnford has not had specific orders to 'reinforce the camp', but Clery is not responsible for Durnford's orders and it is quite likely that he does not know this.

4:00 a.m. Chelmsford has taken personal command of the column which is to reinforce Dartnell. Two ambulances are going with them, but in order to save time the baggage and most of the men's equipment are to be left behind. It is still well before dawn when they march out of camp and towards the Hlazakazi Ridge ten miles to the south-east.

Meanwhile Dartnell and his men, facing what they believe is the main Zulu army, are waiting anxiously for first light. In fact the Zulus in front of them are only the local followers of the chiefs whom the British know as the 'two Matshanas'. A dozen miles away to the north, in the Ngwebeni Valley, Ntshingwayo's main *impi*, 25,000 strong, waits in fitful silence. The night is cold and some of the men sitting among the rocks light fires to warm themselves, but their officers tell them to put them out for fear that they will be spotted by British patrols.[7] The mood is tense, because the Zulus have seen groups of mounted men watching them from a distance as they approached the ravine the previous afternoon, but now they have apparently outwitted the enemy and hidden themselves undetected within a few miles of their camp. Nevertheless, there is little thought of accepting battle in the morning. Wednesday 22 January is the day of the new moon, the 'dead moon' as the Zulus call it, and according to their beliefs it is a very risky day to fight.[8]

Chapter 2

Early Hours

'The horns of the morning.'

———✦———

4:30 a.m.   It is beginning to get light and the Zulus, whose day begins at the time known as the 'horns of the morning' because it is the time when the horns of their cattle are first visible against the sky, are now astir in their bivouacs in the Ngwebeni Valley. Their commanders have reason to be confident. It is true that Ntshingwayo kaMahole does not intend to fight today; not only is the moon inauspicious, but he has orders from Cetshwayo to attempt to negotiate with the British before attacking. Nevertheless, he has already managed to place the bulk of his forces undetected on the British flank. From there they can move forward tomorrow according to the situation as it develops – assuming that the negotiations fail as everyone expects. One possibility is to surround the entire British column if it remains in the camp at Isandlwana, or alternatively the *impi* could descend on it when it is at its most vulnerable as it strikes the camp and resumes its advance. Then, even if Chelmsford's army is too strong to be overwhelmed, there will be a good chance of running off its oxen and horses and leaving it immobilised on the plain. All the regiments which Cetshwayo has sent from oNdini are under Ntshingwayo's direct command in the valley except for three – the uDududu, iMbube and iSangqu, which are destined to form the right horn. They are already moving west across the plateau as the dawn breaks, because Ntshingwayo knows that there is not enough room at the bottom of the ravine to keep the entire *impi* concealed, and has decided to deploy his right wing in a position from where it can threaten the British rear when the time for action finally comes.[1]

5:00 a.m. Lieutenant-Colonel Anthony Durnford is camped with his troops on the Zululand bank of the Mzinyathi River at Rorke's Drift. Durnford is already awake, worried about the state of his wagons, which are suffering from wear and tear after the hard journey up country. There seems no immediate prospect of any action where he is, so as soon as it is light enough he sets off on horseback for Helpmekaar with the idea of obtaining some replacement vehicles from local farmers. He takes with him his transport officer, the 31-year-old Lieutenant William Cochrane, another special service officer seconded from the 32nd Regiment.[2]

6:00 a.m. At Rorke's Drift Lieutenant John Chard is now awake and making plans for the morning. Yesterday he received verbal instructions from Number Three Column to take his engineers up to Isandlwana, but he is not sure whether this also applies to himself. He speaks to his commanding officer, Major Spalding, who has received no orders regarding Chard either. The lieutenant therefore asks permission to go to Isandlwana and see the written orders for himself. He sets out from the mission station on horseback, accompanied by a wagon carrying three sappers and a corporal.[3]

6:30 a.m. Some of the mounted pickets posted on the hills above the escarpment at Isandlwana spot a group of unidentified mounted men moving across the plateau to the north, and return to their officer, Lieutenant Durrant Scott, to report. Scott has set up his headquarters on the conical hill known to the Zulus as Amatutshane, about a mile east of Isandlwana. Scott decides to investigate in person, and rides up onto the plateau.[4]

Mehlokazulu kaSihayo, serving with the iNgobamakhosi regiment, is one of four *izinduna* who have been sent out from their camp in the Ngwebeni Valley at first light to observe the British movements. Now he is stationed on a high point of the escarpment looking down towards Isandlwana. Not far away are the enemy's mounted pickets, but they seem unaware of the small group of Zulus squatting among the rocks. Mehlokazulu can see the lines of tents, the wagons and oxen drawn up behind them, and the comings and goings of bodies of British redcoats and African auxiliaries.[5] What he cannot see is Lord Chelmsford's column, already far away to the east, so he and his companions are unaware that the enemy have divided their forces.

Chelmsford and the mounted elements of his force have ridden ahead and are just now arriving at Dartnell's position, while the infantry and artillery, under the command of Lieutenant-Colonel Degacher, are still on the march in an increasingly strung-out column. The general is greeted by Lieutenant Henry Charles Harford, usually known as Charlie, a young special service officer who has volunteered to serve in Africa on account of his interest in natural history, and is taken to where Dartnell and Rupert Lonsdale are observing the slopes of Magogo Hill to the north-east.

There is a general air of anti-climax; none of the enemy are now visible in the area where camp fires were burning during the night, and Chelmsford quickly ascertains that no Zulus have been sighted since dawn. In fact the Phindo Hills obstruct the view to the east not much more than a mile away, and on the left Magogo similarly conceals a large area of dead ground. To the front, between Dartnell's position and the Phindo Hills, the Mangeni River (which gives its name to the surrounding district) flows south-westward at the bottom of a steep gorge.

To Colonel Glyn the whole position looks far too exposed and dangerous. It has perhaps occurred to him that they might have been deliberately lured into a trap. Surprised that Dartnell has taken the risk of spending the night in a place where he would be so vulnerable, he turns aside for a quiet word with the commander of the 1st Battalion, 3rd NNC, George Hamilton Browne, who is known as 'Maori' on account of his colourful tales of action in New Zealand. 'In God's name Maori, what are you doing here?' he asks. Browne replies with another question; 'In God's name sir, what are you doing here?' to which Glyn responds despairingly 'I am not in command.'[6]

7:00 a.m. As he rides north across the Nqutu Plateau Lieutenant Scott encounters another group of his men coming back towards him. One of them, Trooper Whitelaw, tells him breathlessly that he has just been observing a body of several thousand Zulus moving on the plateau further to the north. It is not clear where they are going, but Scott sends him to Isandlwana at the gallop to alert Colonel Pulleine.[7]

Chelmsford, still determined to seek battle, is issuing his orders to the men at Mangeni.[8] Dartnell is to take the mounted police and volunteers, supported by Hamilton Browne and his NNC, up the Mangeni Valley to the saddle between the Magogo and Phindo Hills, while Russell, with the Imperial Mounted Infantry and the 2nd/3rd NNC, will ride around the rear of Magogo to ensure that no ambush is concealed there. The artillery and the infantry of the 24th will follow Russell as soon as they arrive.

7:20 a.m. Back at Isandlwana the men are having breakfast when Trooper Whitelaw rides in with the message from Scott. A few minutes later a group of Zulus can be seen from the camp on the edge of the plateau, though they quickly retire back over the escarpment. Pulleine reads Whitelaw's report, and although the situation does not appear to be urgent he orders the 'Fall In' to be sounded and begins to deploy his regular companies in line to the east of the camp as a precaution.[9] He sends his isiZulu interpreter, James Brickhill, to tell the wagon drivers to collect and tether the oxen, which might get in the way if they are wandering loose when fighting breaks out. They might also, of course, be run off by parties of Zulus, thus rendering the entire wagon train useless.

Lieutenant Smith-Dorrien rides into Number Two Column's camp at Rorke's Drift with the order that Lieutenant-Colonel Crealock drafted for Lord Chelmsford. Durnford is still on his way to Help-mekaar, but his senior staff officer, Theophilus Shepstone's son George, senses that the message may be urgent. He therefore sends a rider after Durnford with the paper.[10] While he waits for his commanding officer to return, Shepstone orders the tents to be struck so that the column will be ready to march if required. Smith-Dorrien, tired as he is, remounts and returns to Isandlwana for further orders.

7:45 a.m. The rider quickly catches up with Durnford and hands him Chelmsford's order. It puzzles the colonel for several reasons. As we have seen it is ambiguous in several respects; it does not tell him what he is to do when he reaches Isandlwana, and it certainly does not specify who will be in command there. Durnford knows that the general and Colonel Glyn will not be present, so he realises that he will be senior to the officer left in charge. He has in fact been promoted to the rank of brevet colonel, but he does not yet know this, as the notice has not yet reached South Africa from London. Nevertheless, his appointment to the rank of lieutenant-colonel precedes Henry Pulleine's, but he has not been ordered to take command of the troops remaining in the camp. Rather he has been informed that 'artillery and mounted men' are going out to attack the enemy. This in fact is a good description of the composition of his own force, now that most of the infantry have been left behind. Does Crealock envisage that he will be called upon to support Chelmsford's force in the event of a general engagement?

Furthermore the orders for Major Bengough are impossible to implement, as neither Durnford nor Chelmsford knows exactly where he is. He has been delayed on the road, and although he has received the order to move towards the Mzinyathi River at Elands Kraal, he is still just short of the crossing.[11] His battalion, which as things are to turn out might be very useful at either Isandlwana or Rorke's Drift, is stranded between the two battlefields, too far away to assist either.

Durnford has been severely reprimanded once for using his own initiative and he does not want to risk this happening again. On the other hand, he has spent all the years since Bushman's Pass waiting for an opportunity to retrieve his reputation, and he is hardly likely to miss a chance of combat now. He remarks to Lieutenant William Cochrane, who is accompanying him: 'Just what I thought, we are to proceed at once to Isandlwana. There is an impi about eight miles from the camp, which the General moves out to attack at daybreak.' They turn their horses and ride back at once to Rorke's Drift.

The sun is well up in the eastern sky now, and the day is beginning to turn hot. Advancing up the Mangeni valley, Dartnell flushes out a party of about eighty Zulus, who attempt to escape towards the east. The mounted men ride after them and succeed in capturing a few prisoners before the rest disappear among the rocks and caves of the Phindo range. The prisoners are hastily interrogated, but they either cannot or will not supply any useful information on the whereabouts of the main Zulu army.

Major Bengough, leading the 2nd Battalion, 1st NNC, is already on the march and approaching the Mzinyathi River near its confluence with the Isibindi stream about six miles downstream of Rorke's Drift. Here he is surprised to encounter William Beaumont, the commander of the Border Guard – an ad hoc collection of local pro-British Africans whose task it is to alert the authorities to any Zulu threat arising along the border. Beaumont has been out all night looking for a non-existent *impi*, but agrees to guide Bengough across the river.[12]

Lieutenant Chard is still on the road to Isandlwana, unaware of the Zulus massing on his left flank. The wagon is making slow progress on the deeply rutted road, so he rides on ahead to the camp, leaving his men to follow as quickly as they can.

8:00 a.m. Mehlokazulu kaSihayo returns to the Ngwebeni Valley and reports to Ntshingwayo and Mavumengwana, who see no need to change their plan to wait until tomorrow before taking the offensive. 'We will see what they [the British] are going to do,' Ntshingwayo remarks,[13] before calling a council of his leading *izinduna*.

Number Two Column is almost ready to move by the time Durnford returns to Rorke's Drift, and it starts out on the road to Isandlwana, leaving Lieutenant Cochrane to organise the wagons and follow on. Cochrane is still unsure what his commanding officer is thinking, but he believes that the column is going into action and is anxious not to be left behind.[14]

8:05 a.m. No further enemy have been seen from the camp at Isandlwana for half an hour, but Pulleine sends a message to Chelmsford warning

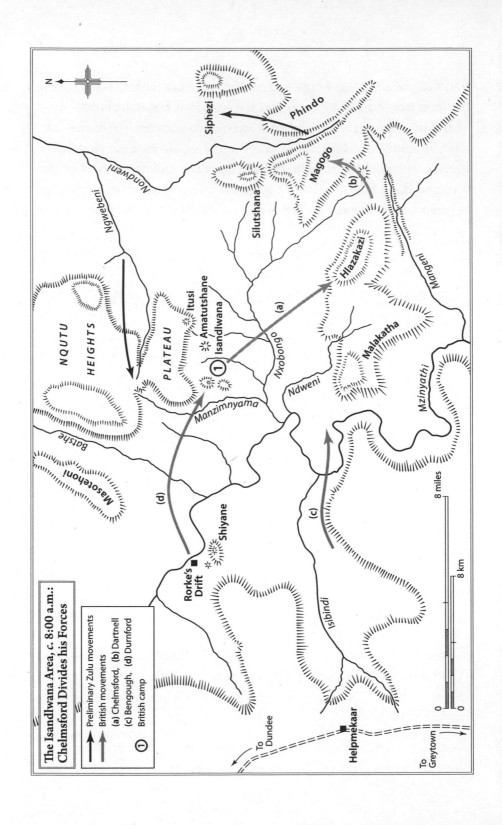

N

Phindo

Siphezi

Magogo

Ngwebeni

Nondweni

Silutshana

Hlazakazi

(b)

Amatutshane

Ittusi

Isandlwana

NQUTU

PLATEAU

(a)

Malakatha

HEIGHTS

Nxobongo

Ndweni

Mzinyathi

Manzimnyama

Batshe

Masotehoni

(d)

(c)

Shiyane

Rorke's
Drift

Isibindi

Helpmekaar

To
Dundee

To
Greytown

8 miles

8 km

0

0

The Isandlwana Area, c. 8:00 a.m.:
Chelmsford Divides his Forces

Preliminary Zulu movements
British movements
(a) Chelmsford, (b) Dartnell
(c) Bengough, (d) Durnford
① British camp

him that the Zulus have been sighted and are 'advancing in force from left front of camp'.[15] The men are still standing to, but there is no sense of imminent danger. Lieutenant Henry Curling, who is standing to with his guns, will later recall that, 'We none of us had the least idea that the Zulus contemplated attacking the camp and, having in the last war [the Cape Frontier War of the previous year] often seen equally large bodies of the enemy, never dreamed they would come on.'[16]

8:30 a.m. Captain Barry, the commander of a group of NNC who are acting as advanced sentries on Mkwene Hill, up on the Nqutu plateau, observe large numbers of Zulus manoeuvring in the distance. They appear to be in three separate columns, totalling several thousand men. Two of these columns seem to be moving off towards the north-east, away from the camp, but the third goes westward and is lost to sight behind Isandlwana Hill. Luckily for Barry's men the enemy do not spot them, and their officer sends Lieutenant Gert Adendorff back to Colonel Pulleine with another urgent report.[17]

Chapter 3

Late Morning

'Zulus retire everywhere. Men fall out for dinner.'
(from Lieutenant Pope's diary, discovered after the battle)

———◆◆———

9:00 a.m. The NNC troops with Chelmsford's force, having cleared Magogo Hill, are beginning to advance towards the Phindo Hills across the gorge, watched by the general and his staff through field glasses.

Chard arrives at Isandlwana and reports to headquarters, where he finds a copy of his orders and discovers that his own presence is not required, and that his responsibility is still for the ponts and the road between the Mzinyathi and Helpmekaar. He therefore prepares to return without delay to his post at Rorke's Drift.[1]

Lieutenant Adendorff arrives in the camp at Isandlwana with Barry's message for Pulleine. Adendorff is not a professional soldier, and what is more his first language is German, not English. Consequently his report is not very clear,[2] and another of the NNC officers in camp, Lieutenant Walter Higginson, rides up to the plateau to investigate.

9:15 a.m. As Chelmsford's two NNC battalions advance up the slopes of Phindo Hill they come under fire from several hundred Zulus stationed along the crest, and men start to fall. Henry Harford, temporarily in command in the absence of Commandant Lonsdale, who has galloped off in pursuit of a fleeing Zulu, rallies the men in a sheltered position, then despatches them by companies to work around the flanks while he leads the remainder forward.[3] In contrast to their panicky mood last night the NNC seem to be in good spirits and eager for action. At one spot thirteen men are shot one after the other by Zulu snipers, and Harford has to go up and stop their comrades continuing the

The edge of the Nqutu Plateau seen from the vicinity of the camp at Isandlwana. It was somewhere along the edge of this escarpment that Lieutenant Chard and others saw part of the Zulu right horn moving into position at about 9:15.

suicidal advance. It helps that he was brought up in South Africa and speaks fluent isiZulu. Despite the heavy fire Harford is miraculously untouched. Elsewhere on the hill he personally shoots a Zulu who has been holding up his men at a range of about thirty yards. The war correspondent Charles Norris Newman, watching from the vicinity of Chelmsford's command post, is greatly impressed by the young officer's courage and initiative.[4] His fellow officers can almost forgive him for his greatest faux pas to date – the misuse of a bottle of gin to preserve a specimen of a rare species of beetle.

Before Chard sets out from the camp he notices large numbers of men moving on the rim of the Tahelane Spur, a projection of the plateau which runs roughly north-east to south-west only a thousand yards from the closest of the tents. He borrows 'a field glass' (possibly a telescope) from an NCO, and through it he can see that they are Zulus; many of them are moving westward, to Chard's left, until they are lost to view behind the looming bulk of Isandlwana. None of them appear to be a threat to the camp at present; in fact Chard's conclusion is that they might be planning to attack his ponts at Rorke's Drift, so he decides to hurry back before they can cut the road.[5]

A brief outburst of firing from the east is heard by some among the Zulus waiting in the Ngwebeni Valley, probably emanating from Chelmsford's column. However, the source of the sound is uncertain and a rumour spreads among the other regiments that the iNgobamakhosi – who have a reputation as glory hunters – have disobeyed orders and become involved in a fight. In fact the iNgobamakhosi are too busy cooking breakfast to take much notice of the firing, but many of their neighbours, the uNokhenkhe and uKhandempemvu regiments, leave the camp and run up onto the plateau to see what is happening, reluctant to leave their rivals to win all the glory.[6] When they realise that the iNgobamakhosi have not moved, and that there is no sign of any fighting on their front, they begin to disperse or return to their positions in the valley.

On Mkwene Hill Higginson finds Barry's men observing the movements of a group of Zulus about a mile away, with other enemy units visible further off to the left. He can only guess at their identity, but in fact the nearest of the Zulus are skirmishers screening part of the detached right horn of the army, which comprises the uDududu, iMbube and iSangqu regiments. The iSangqu, or 'Hunters', are the oldest, born around 1828 and thus around fifty years old. They are married men whose senior status is advertised by their mainly white shields. The iMbube, the 'Lions', and the uDududu, whose name derives from the war cry of advancing warriors, are around ten years younger, and carry black shields with white spots. Some of the men glimpsed further off may be part of the uNokhenkhe and uKhandempemvu returning to their places after the false alarm. They do not seem to be advancing towards the camp, so Higginson watches them for about half an hour and then returns to report to Pulleine.[7]

The rider bearing Colonel Pulleine's 8:05 message reaches Chelmsford, who does not appear to appreciate its significance. He reads it and hands it to Major Clery without comment. Clery asks him for instructions and receives the reply, 'There is nothing to be done on that.'[8] However, the general does send for a naval officer attached to his staff, Lieutenant Berkeley Milne, and orders him to climb a nearby hill, accompanied by Captain Symons of D Company 1st/24th, and observe the camp at Isandlwana with his powerful telescope.

9:20 a.m. Then Chelmsford, still preoccupied with what is happening to the east, decides that it is time to resume the advance. He sends Captain Alan Gardner from Glyn's staff with orders to Pulleine to strike camp and bring his force up to join him. Several other young officers, including Lieutenants Dyer of the 2nd/24th and Second Lieutenant Thomas Griffith of the transport staff, go with Gardner to help oversee the move, and Colonel Harness sends back his second-in-command, Major Smith, to look after the rest of N Battery. As there will also be a need for additional labour to assist the regulars in packing up the camp, Chelmsford sends a messenger to Hamilton Browne to bring his NNC battalion back to his command post to receive fresh orders.[9]

James Brickhill, still doing the rounds of the transport drivers on the higher ground of the nek at Isandlwana, notices sentries signalling the approach of troops up the road from Rorke's Drift, and returns to report this to Pulleine.[10]

9:30 a.m. A messenger sent by Higginson from Mkwene Hill reaches Pulleine, who decides that it may become necessary to deny the commanding height of the Tahelane Spur to the enemy. He orders Lieutenant Cavaye to take his E Company, 1st/24th, up the escarpment and occupy it.[11]

The men arriving from Rorke's Drift turn out to be Durnford's column, which Chard meets on the road. He informs Durnford of what he has seen on the spur, and the colonel asks him to pass on the message as he rides past the column. Following behind them Chard finds his four men with the wagon. He orders the sappers to go ahead on foot with Durnford's men, while he and Driver Robson take the wagon back to Rorke's Drift. Inadvertently, therefore, he saves Robson's life while sending the others to their deaths.

9:45 a.m. Lord Chelmsford's messenger locates Hamilton Browne, whose men are currently exchanging fire with Zulu skirmishers on the Phindo Hills. Browne has first to locate his colleague, Cooper of the 2nd/3rd NNC, and inform him that he is being left to carry on the fight on his own, then extricate his own men and ride back to Chelmsford's command post to find out why he is being recalled. He embarks on this seemingly pointless task with growing irritation; as his earlier exchange with Colonel Glyn has emphasised, he is beginning to lose any confidence which he might have had in the way the campaign is being run.[12]

9:55 a.m. E Company reaches the top of the Tahelane Spur and finds it unoccupied. Cavaye deploys his men in skirmish order, taking cover behind the rocks that are scattered over the plateau. On his right he can see Mkwene Hill, where Barry's NNC are also taking cover. There is a gap of several hundred yards between the two units, but at least he cannot be taken by surprise from that direction. To the front he has a good field of fire extending for about a thousand yards, but the steep drop at the south-western end of the spur prevents him seeing into the Manzimnyama Valley below, where the Zulus might be able to approach the camp without being seen. Therefore Cavaye sends Second Lieutenant Dyson out to the left to a point from where he can keep the valley under observation.[13] There is still no sign of the enemy.

10:00 a.m. Hamilton Browne's arrival interrupts Lord Chelmsford and his staff at breakfast. On being asked by the general if he has eaten, an increasingly annoyed Browne replies that he has not, and neither have his men.[14] He goes on to enquire if his commander knows that he was engaged with the enemy when he was called away. Colonel

Looking south-west from the top of the escarpment towards the Tahelane Spur and Rorke's Drift. The level plateau on the right is where Lieutenant Cavaye's E Company was deployed just before 10 a.m., and its retreat just after midday took it down the slope in the foreground towards the left.

Crealock then rescues Chelmsford by issuing Browne with his orders before he can become even more insubordinate. He is to march back to Isandlwana, pack up the camp and then return before nightfall. No mention is made of the enemy, but Browne knows that they are nearby in unknown strength. What is more his men have not been fed for the last twenty-four hours and his white NCOs, unaccustomed to marching on foot across the African terrain, are close to exhaustion. But he realises that he can hardly argue with Crealock, so he simply salutes and asks 'If I come across the enemy?' Crealock's reply typifies his careless underestimation of the Zulu threat. 'Oh, just brush them aside and go on,' he says. The colonel then returns to his breakfast, leaving Browne speechless.

Durnford rides into the camp at Isandlwana with his mounted units. Still somewhere behind him on the road, moving at the speed of men on foot, are the supply wagons, rocket battery and supporting NNC infantry that are attached to his column. The infantry in the camp are still under arms, but all now seems to be quiet. Durnford tells his men to dismount and unsaddle their horses, then goes in search of Pulleine. William Cochrane, who is with Durnford, witnesses the meeting between the two men, at which he believes that his commanding officer has formally taken command of the camp.[15] Durnford receives an oral report from Pulleine, who repeats several times that he has orders from Lord Chelmsford to defend the position. He is clearly worried that Durnford will countermand these orders, but in fact the latter has no idea at this point of what to do. He has been expecting further orders from the commander-in-chief to be waiting for him, but there are none. He does not know whether he is intended to reinforce the defenders of the camp or continue to operate as the commander of an independent column. His first priority is to establish what is happening on his left flank, so he interrogates Lieutenant Higginson, who has just come back from his trip to Barry's position. Higginson, however, can give him no clear picture of what the Zulus are doing, so Durnford decides to post lookouts on top of Isandlwana Hill. He is unaware of the fact that the summit does not overlook the plateau but is slightly lower, so that these men will be able to see nothing of any enemy movements to the north.

10:10 a.m. Lieutenant Milne returns to Chelmsford and reports that he can see nothing of significance around the camp except for some oxen moving on the saddle. Chelmsford takes no further action.

10:30 a.m. Durnford has heard nothing from the men on Isandlwana Hill, so he orders Higginson to send a messenger to bring down a report at once. The man can discover nothing useful, but he is under pressure not to disappoint the impatient Durnford, so he gives him his best guess, which is that the enemy are retiring. Lieutenant Cochrane, remaining within earshot of Durnford, hears scouts come in from the plateau with various reports – that the Zulus are indeed retiring, that they are concentrating behind the hills, and even that they have split into two columns, one of which is moving east, towards Chelmsford's position.[16] The lieutenant is sceptical about some of these reports, noting that the messenger who claims that the enemy are in retreat is not wearing any sort of uniform and his credentials are uncertain, but it is impossible from the perspective of the camp to know what is happening. In fact Ntshingwayo's men still have no orders to move against either of the British forces, but Durnford is concerned about the vulnerability, not of the camp, but of his commander-in-chief, who it seems might be attacked in the rear by the enemy who are moving in his direction while he is already engaged to his front.

10:35 a.m. The discussion between Durnford and Pulleine becomes increasingly heated, with a great deal of gesturing towards the north and east, and several junior officers in the vicinity are gradually drawn in. Cochrane hears Durnford announce that he will go out and intercept the Zulus, while his colleague repeats that he cannot allow his infantry to join him as he is under strict orders to hold the camp. Durnford then asks for the loan of two companies, at which Lieutenant Teignmouth Melvill, the 1st Battalion's Adjutant, intervenes in his superior's support, telling Durnford, 'I really do not think Colonel Pulleine would be doing right to send any men out of the camp.' Durnford replies 'Very well, it does not much matter, we will not take them.' However, he continues, 'My idea is that wherever Zulus appear, we ought to attack.'[17] Adding that he will expect Pulleine to support him if he gets into trouble, he prepares to move out with his own column.

10:50. Durnford's rocket battery and its infantry escort finally struggle into camp, already tired by their long march. The wagons are still on the road behind them. As there is still no sign of the enemy, Pulleine orders the men who have been standing to in front of the camp since breakfast time to fall out and prepare their dinners.

Meanwhile Durnford leaves Isandlwana and advances eastward with his cavalry. He has not given any thought to how Pulleine's slower-moving infantry will be able to assist him if he needs them, and does not even wait for his own rocket battery to catch up, simply ordering it to follow as best it can. He sends one troop of Zikhali's Horse under Lieutenant Vause back to bring in the wagons, and orders Lieutenants Raw and Roberts with the remaining two troops of Zikhali's, accompanied by George Shepstone, to ride out to the north onto the plateau. Their instructions are to pick up Barry's NNC and continue behind the hill known as Itusi, with the apparent intention of securing the flank of the rest of the force as it moves eastward before rejoining it somewhere nearer to Mangeni.[18]

11:10 a.m. Raw and Roberts have a long way to go and have pushed their horses hard. They arrive at Barry's position on Mkwene Hill and pass on Durnford's order. Barry's men follow the cavalry as best they can.

The last of the uNokhenkhe and uKhandempemvu regiments are only now being rallied by their officers in the Ngwebeni Valley after the earlier false alarm, and Ntshingwayo and his senior commanders are still conferring about their battle plan for tomorrow.[19] At about the same time a patrol of the Natal Carbineers, sent out by Lieutenant Scott from his post on Amatutshane, spots some of the Zulu left wing in the north-eastern part of the Ngwebeni Valley and returns to report, but the Zulus have not seen them and do not react.

11:30 a.m. Durnford rides past Itusi with his mounted troops and disappears out of sight of the camp. Meanwhile Raw and Roberts are riding across the plateau towards the Ngwebeni Valley, scattering small groups of Zulu foragers as they go. They spot some of the enemy trying to drive a herd of cattle away into the valley, and Raw's troop gallops after them. Suddenly they reach the crest of a ridge and stare in amazement at 15,000 Zulus sitting quietly in ordered ranks below them.[20] They have only seconds to take in the scene, but all the regiments of the Zulu centre and left horn are spread out along the valley. Among those nearest to them are the warriors of the uKhandempemvu regiment, also known as the umCijo; the names mean 'black and white marked head', or 'needle pointed at both ends' respectively. Their unit was formed by Cetshwayo in 1868, so they are aged around thirty. The precise patterns on their shields vary from company to company, but most are black or dark brown with large white patches. The neighbouring uNokhenkhe ('a unit running out of control', perhaps implying youthful impetuosity) was recruited from the age set before theirs, so its men are a couple of years older. Their shields are brown with large white patches. Next in line is the uMbonambi regiment, whose name means 'those who experience sorrow'. They are in their mid-thirties and carry mottled black and white shields. Further away are the iNgobamakhosi, young men in their mid-twenties; they were formed and given their impressive title, the 'humblers of kings', seven years ago. They carry shields in a variety of colours – mostly brown, but some black or spotted with white. Lastly there are the uVe, or 'flycatchers', who are named after the small woodland birds that dart restlessly to and fro in pursuit of their insect prey; these warriors are in their early twenties, and their youthful eagerness and physical fitness has obviously suggested the comparison. Their shield colours are mostly shades of reddish brown, some with white markings.

The cavalrymen, silhouetted against the sky, are spotted at once. The men of the uNokhenhke and uKhandempemvu, already in a state of excitement after their previous excursion, are the first to react. Without waiting for orders they spring to their feet and rush towards the enemy, shouting 'This is the king's day!'[21] Raw's men fire a volley, which brings down a few of the Zulus but alerts many more to the danger, and the men of the uMbonambi, iNgobamakhosi and uVe, bivouacked further to the east, also rise and run forward. Lieutenant Roberts brings his men up at the gallop to support Raw, and as the Zulus pour over the ridge both troops begin to fall back, halting at intervals to fire further volleys.

The uDududu, iSangqu and iMbube regiments on the right are already in position north of the Tahelane Spur, much closer to the British position than their comrades in the Ngwebeni Valley. Their officers hear the firing from the centre and run up to vantage points on the ridges surrounding them, from which they can see the units of the chest pouring out of the valley. They know what their traditional battle drill requires them to do in this situation, and so without waiting for orders they gesture their men forward. Their intention is to make a wide sweep around Isandlwana Hill and outflank the enemy left.[22]

Henry Pulleine, back at Isandlwana, can hear the sound of firing breaking out at several points on the plateau to the north. He hurriedly drafts an order to Lieutenant Cavaye on the Tahelane Spur:

> Cavaye,
>   Zulus are advancing on your right in force. Retire on camp in order. E Coy will support your left. H N Pulleine. 11:30 a.m.[23]

He entrusts this message to his adjutant, Lieutenant Melvill. Cavaye's position is well beyond the rim of the escarpment and so is not visible from the camp, but Melvill urges his horse up the steep slope, guided by the sound of firing. Behind him Captain William Mostyn and F Company (who are presumably who Pulleine means by 'E Company', as the latter are already in position) follow at the double. Pulleine also sends Curling with the two artillery pieces out to a position on top of a low rocky ridge, 400 yards away to the east; he is probably thinking that from there they can give support to Durnford if necessary, while also having a good field of fire to the north. Curling is briefly excited at the prospect of commanding the guns himself, but at the last minute Major Smith appears to take over.[24] As the two guns cannot be expected to hold their position unsupported, A Company 1st/24th will accompany them. The officer placed in command of this company is Captain William Degacher, acting Major of the 1st Battalion and brother of Lieutenant-Colonel Henry, who is out at Mangeni with Lord Chelmsford.

In fact Cavaye is already in action. As the sound of firing breaks out from the right, a large body of Zulus suddenly emerges half a mile to his front, and moves steadily across from right to left across the top of the spur in the direction of the Manzimnyama Valley. The British do not know it, but this is part of the right horn commencing its outflanking manoeuvre. Cavaye orders his men to fire a volley. The practice of firing as a unit on a word of command, rather than individually, is designed not only to maximise the impact on the enemy and exert some control over ammunition expenditure, but also to allow time for the smoke from the rifles to clear so that the target is not obscured. It does, however, have the disadvantage of allowing a few seconds after each round of firing during which the enemy is relatively safe and able to react. Several of the enemy fall to this first volley, and Cavaye expects their comrades to wheel around and charge his position, but to his surprise they simply keep going across his front, similarly ignoring further volleys sent in their direction, until they disappear from sight.[25]

Lieutenant Chard returns to Rorke's Drift and informs Major Spalding of what he has seen on the road, and the potential threat from the Zulu forces manoeuvring to the north. For the first time he sees Spalding's 'Order of the Day', which was issued while he was at Isandlwana. It informs him that Captain Rainforth's G Company of the 1st/24th has been ordered up from Helpmekaar to defend the ponts at the drift in the absence of Durnford's column, and that in the meantime the position will be entrusted to an NCO and six privates from Bromhead's company, supported by fifty of Captain Stevenson's NNC. However, there is still no sign of Rainforth, and in the light of Chard's information Major Spalding realises that the ponts will be very vulnerable if an attack materialises. He decides to go back towards Helpmekaar himself to find out what has happened to G Company.[26]

1.35 a.m. Ntshingwayo and his officers have no chance to halt the movement of their regiments now that the enemy is in sight, but they do manage to organise them into an improvised battle formation in accordance with the Zulu 'horns of the bull' doctrine. The uNokhenkhe, uMbonambi and uKhandempemvu become the centre or chest, while the iNgobamakhosi and uVe form the left horn, tasked with outflanking the enemy on that side. Only the Undi corps, consisting of the married veterans of the uThulwana, iNdlondlo, uDloko and iNdluyengwe regiments, do not join in the general advance. They have been stationed to the east, well away from the spot where Raw's men appeared, and their officers have managed to restrain them. Ntshingwayo stands amongst them now singing the praises of Shaka and his father Senzangakhona, and warning them 'There is no going back home.'[27] But neither, yet, does he lead them forward. They will be the loins of the army, the elite held in reserve for emergencies.

Barry's NNC, still advancing across the plateau behind Raw and Roberts' cavalry, suddenly see them falling back, hard-pressed by the skirmishers of the Zulu chest. What is worse, they can also see the Zulu right horn massing on their left flank, in the direction of the Tahelane Spur. They realise their peril at once and break in rout, fleeing towards Isandlwana.

George Shepstone breaks away from the fight on the plateau to take the news to Colonel Pulleine, galloping hard towards a notch in the escarpment not far from Amatutshane, where the descent is relatively easy.

Lieutenant Scott's patrol gallops back to his post on top of Amatutshane to report the sighting which they made just before Raw triggered the avalanche. Scott can now see the Zulu left horn coming across the plateau, and sends a party of his Carbineers to ride after Durnford and warn him.[28] Durnford is still clearly visible from Amatutshane, moving steadily eastward, but from his position on the lower ground he can still see only a few skirmishers retiring ahead of him.

11:40 a.m. Smith and Curling arrive at their new position and unlimber the guns. From here they can observe to their right as far the Nyogane donga, a deep ravine which runs north to south across the plain about 700 yards east of the camp, and to their left the section of the escarpment down which the Zulu chest is about to come. Directly ahead, the conical hill of Amatutshane is about 1,200 yards away. The infantrymen of A Company come up and deploy behind them and on either flank so as not to obstruct their field of fire.

Even when the breathless riders catch up with Durnford and deliver Scott's warning he dismisses the danger, simply remarking, 'The enemy

Looking north towards the plateau from near the location of British firing line.
To the right is the 'notch' in the escarpment down which the uKhandempemvu
and uMbonambi regiments descended to surprise Durnford's rocket battery.
Amatutshane Hill is just out of view on the right.

can't surround us and if they do we will cut a way through them.'[29] He
then tells the Carbineers to return with a message to Scott to bring up
his picket to join him, but they reply that their officer has orders from
Pulleine not to leave his post. Durnford's irritated response is that he is
senior to Pulleine and that Scott must obey his orders.

Interlude

'Gentlemen in England now abed . . .'

———◆◆◆———

Six thousand miles away at the royal residence at Osborne House on the Isle of Wight, on the south coast of England, the weather is bitterly cold, made worse by strong winds blowing from the east. It has been like this for several days, and it is exacerbating Queen Victoria's dismal mood. She is spending the day resting and writing, still very preoccupied with the recent death of her daughter Princess Alice, who succumbed to diphtheria in December.[1] Alice's children have come to visit her, and she has taken the opportunity to interrogate her daughter's dresser, Mary Adams, at length about her recollections of her mistress' final days. The Queen's thoughts are far from events in Zululand, and it will be nearly three weeks before news of the day's doings reaches London.

The readers of the British newspapers this morning are no more preoccupied than their sovereign with the distant war in South Africa.[2] Under the heading 'The War with the Zulus', the *Derby Mercury* quotes from 'the Capetown papers' Sir Bartle Frere's ultimatum to Cetshwayo issued in December, but has no news of subsequent events. The *Exeter Flying Post* cites a pamphlet issued by Lord Chelmsford, 'who is now on the Zulu border', which gives 'much information concerning the order in which the Zulus march, their mode of crossing rivers, and the tactics which regulate their movements in the field'. But the headlines are dominated by affairs closer to home. According to the London *Daily News*, the easterly wind has prevented the Harwich fishing fleet from sailing and added to the 'considerable distress' already inflicted on that town by the economic depression. The *Glasgow Herald* gives prominence to the trial at Edinburgh of the directors and manager of the City of Glasgow Bank, who are charged with falsifying the company's balance sheet. The bank collapsed in October 1878, ruining many of its shareholders, and this is the third day of a trial which is expected to last another week.

The *Coventry Times*, serving the county of Warwickshire where the 24th Foot is notionally based, warns its readers against an improved version of the longstanding menace of horse theft, which involves a man dressed to impersonate a wagon driver making away with horse, wagon and contents while the rightful owner is visiting a customer. Drivers are advised that if they encounter a man on foot dressed exactly like themselves, they should not regard the imitation as 'the sincerest form of flattery', but instead be on their guard. The same publication quotes an attack on the 'Incompetency and Untruthfulness of the Tory Ministry' by a speaker at a Liberal meeting in Manchester, but the 'nefarious war' which the government is accused of entering into 'without any justification whatsoever' is that which began last November in Afghanistan. The Afghan War is also the main news story in the *Naval and Military Gazette* of London, along with the explosion on board the ironclad HMS *Thunderer*, one of whose 12-inch muzzle-loading guns recently burst during firing practice.

Meanwhile, even as Ntshingwayo's warriors are sweeping forward to envelop Lord Chelmsford's camp, the Zulus and everyone else in southern Africa are being outflanked strategically on the grandest imaginable scale. In an office in distant Brussels Henry Morton Stanley, famous as the rescuer of David Livingstone and explorer of the Congo River, is completing his plans for a return to the Congo.[3] He came back to Europe late in 1877 full of enthusiasm for developing and administering the new lands and peoples that he had 'discovered', but the British government was less keen on the expenditure involved, so he took employment instead with King Leopold II of the Belgians. Leopold had long been looking for a colony for himself, and he set Stanley to work to establish one in the vast unclaimed centre of Africa. The French explorer Pierre Savorgnan de Brazza also came back from Central Africa about three weeks ago, and the possibility of him leading a rival French expedition has given a new urgency to Stanley's work. In August 1879 Stanley will be back in Africa. Within a few years the rapids that have always prevented navigation on the Congo will be circumvented by a railway, steamers will ply its upper reaches – and as a consequence, albeit unintended by Stanley, millions of Congolese will be condemned to decades of brutal exploitation.[4] In the long term Leopold's move will set off a land grab that will only end when almost the whole of Africa has been divided among the European powers. Never again will the peoples of southern Africa have the option of retreating from their opponents and taking refuge in the unexplored north. But for now, retreat is the last thing on the Zulus' minds.

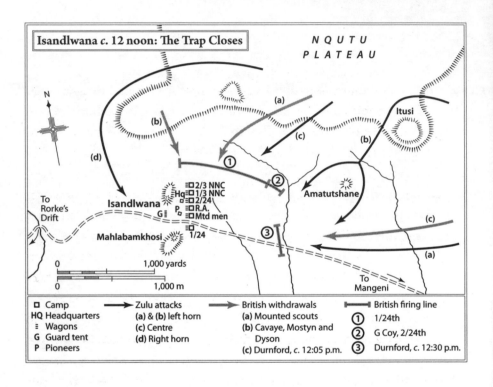

Isandlwana *c.* 12 noon: The Trap Closes

N Q U T U
P L A T E A U

N

Itusi

(a)

(b)

(c)

(b)

(d)

(1)

(2)

Amatutshane

To
Rorke's
Drift

Isandlwana

⊟ 2/3 NNC
Hq ⊟ 1/3 NNC
□ ⊟ 2/24
P □ ⊟ R.A.
G ⊟ □ ⊟ Mtd men

(c)

(a)

Mahlabamkhosi

⊟
1/24

(3)

0   1,000 yards

0   1,000 m

To
Mangeni

□ Camp	→ Zulu attacks	► British withdrawals	⊢━┥ British firing line
HQ Headquarters	**(a) & (b)** left horn	**(a)** Mounted scouts	① 1/24th
⋮ Wagons	**(c)** Centre	**(b)** Cavaye, Mostyn and	② G Coy, 2/24th
G Guard tent	**(d)** Right horn	Dyson	③ Durnford, *c.* 12:30 p.m.
P Pioneers		**(c)** Durnford, *c.* 12:05 p.m.	

Chapter 4

High Noon

'I was surprised how relaxed the men in the ranks
were . . .' *(Edward Essex)*

————◆◆◆————

12 noon. Teignmouth Melvill arrives on top of the spur to discover that
the senior officer on that part of the front is not Cavaye but Captain
Essex of the 75th Foot, who is serving as Director of Transport for
Number Three Column. Having no other pressing duties at the time
Essex was in his tent writing letters when he heard Cavaye's men open
fire. On learning from a sergeant that the company on the spur was
under attack he has ridden out on his own initiative to find out what
is happening.[1] He has picked up his revolver, though realising the need
for haste he has not stopped to put on his sword, but left it in his tent.
Melvill delivers Pulleine's message to Essex, who realises that there is
a risk that Second Lieutenant Dyson's detachment, which is still in its
isolated position on the far left, will be abandoned in a withdrawal. He
therefore rides off to give Dyson the retire order in person. Meanwhile
Mostyn's men deploy in the gap between Cavaye and Dyson. Barry's
demoralised NNC are now streaming past them and down the spur
towards the camp. To the front of Cavaye and Mostyn all is quiet
again, but the threat from the right is developing rapidly as the advance
skirmishers of the uNokhenkhe come into sight.

　　Lieutenant Walter Stafford and his fifty NNC also arrive on top of
the spur and are directed into position to extend the line on Mostyn's left
flank.[2] In front of them, at a range of about 800 yards, Stafford can see
large numbers of Zulus who are either moving forward or sitting down;
the former are presumably the uNokhenkhe skirmishers, advancing

through elements of one of the regiments of the right horn which has yet to catch up with the rest of the formation. One of Stafford's African NCOs approaches and asks him how to adjust the sight of his rifle. There can be no better example of the unpreparedness of many of the NNC than this: they have not learned how to carry out such a basic procedure until the enemy are actually in sight. Nevertheless, with commendable patience, Stafford demonstrates it for the man. He takes the weapon, sets the sight to 700 yards and fires. The round has obviously fallen short, so he puts the sight up to 800 yards and tries again. This time he sees the bullet hit one of the Zulus, and he hands the rifle back to the NCO, though without much hope that he can use it effectively when the range closes. Essex notes that others of the NNC are blazing away 'at an absurd rate', depleting their ammunition without having any effect on the distant enemy.

Durnford is still arguing with Scott's Carbineers when some of his men interrupt to tell him that the enemy is in sight. The officers all look towards the low ridge that rises in front of them, slightly less than a mile to the east. Over it come what seem like thousands of Zulus, in skirmish order according to William Cochrane, ten or twelve men deep.[3] This is the uVe regiment, the Flycatchers, who have covered the ground between the Ngwebeni Valley and the edge of the escarpment at a run. Durnford realises in a split second that he has seriously underestimated what he is up against, but he keeps his nerve and issues his orders in a calm and precise manner. As the range closes to 800 yards some of the uVe open fire, but they are still far beyond the effective range of their muskets.

12:05 p.m. Durnford waits until the range has halved to 400 yards before he orders his troopers to return the fire of the uVe, then organises an orderly retirement with each troop alternately moving and halting to fire.[4]

As well as his messengers to Durnford, Scott has sent men back to the camp to alert Pulleine. On the way they meet Major Russell with Durnford's rocket battery, still out on their own on the open plain.

The troopers advise Russell to join Scott on top of Amatutshane, but like his commanding officer he has no idea of the scale or speed of the enemy advance, and instead proposes to turn to his left and go up the escarpment in search of targets for his rockets.[5] The major, who has a horse, rides on ahead up the notch where Shepstone came down, and reaches the top while his men and the mules carrying the rockets are still only half way up. He almost runs into the advance skirmishers of the iNgobamakhosi, who are coming straight towards him, having covered the three miles or so from the Ngwebeni Valley in less than half an hour. An astonished Russell wheels and gallops back down the hill, shouting to his men to get the rockets into action.[6] The crew manage to place the first rocket into its trough and fire just as the Zulus appear over the edge of the escarpment a few hundred yards ahead. The 9-pounder rockets are unpredictable in flight and carry no explosive charge apart from any propellant not consumed before the target, so apart from their effectiveness at starting fires they are mainly a psychological weapon, intended to intimidate with their noise and flame. This one flies over the heads of the enemy and out of sight; a few of the Zulus are burned by the sparks, but although startled they are far from demoralised, and their advance is not checked. A praise singer among the iNgobamakhosi hurriedly improvises a verse to stiffen their morale, playing on the similarity between the isiZulu word for 'heaven' and the name of the Zulu people themselves:

> Lightning of heaven, it glitters and shines. The sun of the amaZulu, it consumes all![7]

The iNgobamakhosi respond by advancing to within about a hundred yards, lying down and firing a volley, then advancing again shouting '*Usuthu!*' The terrified mules flee with the remaining rockets, followed by most of the NNC escort. Major Russell is shot and falls from his horse; Captain Nourse, commanding the NNC, helps him to mount again, but soon afterwards Russell is hit once more and killed. Luckily for Nourse the enemy skirmishers continue to fire from a distance instead of closing, content to wait for their supports to come up, and the captain manages to rally some of his men and make a stand by a pile of rocks.[8] Meanwhile the survivors of the rocket crew, Bombardiers Gough and Grant and Privates Johnson and Trainer, make their escape in the direction of the camp. Gough and Grant have managed to grab a couple of mules and mount them, but their two comrades are forced to flee on foot.

Major Spalding is about to ride out of the Rorke's Drift post when a thought strikes him. All is quiet at the moment, but if anything does happen there needs to be a clear chain of command in his absence. He calls to Chard 'Which of you is senior, you or Bromhead?'[9] Chard does not know; the two officers are from different branches of the service and the question of either of them taking overall command has not arisen until now. So Spalding has to dismount and go back to his tent, where he consults his copy of the Army List. Chard's commission, he notes, predates Bromhead's by a few months. 'I see you are senior', he tells Chard, 'so you will be in charge, although of course nothing will happen, and I shall be back again early this evening.' Then he rides off, leaving Chard to have a leisurely lunch and retire to his tent to write some letters home.

12:15 p.m. Durnford and his men fall back round the slope of Amatutshane and find Nourse and the four of his companions who are still on their feet exchanging fire at a distance with the iNgobamakhosi. The troopers try to collect some of the mules with their cargo of rockets, but quickly abandon the idea as their pursuers close in. Instead, they continue their retreat, taking Nourse and his men with them.

Captain Alan Gardner rides into the camp with the order from Chelmsford. He rode past Amatutshane just moments before the Zulus arrived at the edge of the escarpment, and is still unaware of the disaster unfolding over to his right. He finds Pulleine and hands over his message.[10] The colonel is instructed to strike the camp and march to join the commander-in-chief with seven day's worth of rations, leaving behind only a small detachment to guard those stores which cannot be taken. Pulleine reads the paper with mounting frustration.

This is the second time in an hour that he has received orders which he cannot comply with. First Durnford tells him to move in his support, contradicting his instructions from Chelmsford to defend the camp, and now the general is telling him to move, at precisely the time when the outbreak of firing to the north makes this impossible.

At this point George Shepstone gallops up with the alarming news that the Zulus are advancing towards the escarpment in force and 'fast driving our men this way'. James Brickhill notes that for a moment Pulleine looks 'totally nonplussed'.[11] Shepstone and Gardner both urge him not to take any chances. Shepstone emphasises that the Zulus are driving Zikhali's horse and the NNC back towards the camp, and that the retreating men will need urgent support. Gardner goes further. 'I should advise your disobeying the general's orders, for the present at any rate,' he tells Pulleine. He adds that Chelmsford knows nothing of the attack on the camp, but is aware only of the behaviour of the Zulus facing him at Mangeni, who seem to be trying to avoid battle.

So Pulleine composes a hasty note to the general and hands it to a dispatch rider: 'Heavy firing to left of camp. Cannot move camp at present. H B Pulleine, Lt Col.' 'Left' is a reference to the orientation of the camp facing the east, so Pulleine clearly has in mind the sounds of Raw and Roberts's volleys coming from the escarpment to the north. He then orders Gardner to go with him and assist him in deploying his troops. The captain adds an explanatory note of his own, based on what he has observed, and sends the messenger hurrying back to Chelmsford. 'Heavy firing to the left of camp' he repeats, 'Shepstone has come in for reinforcements and reports that the Basutos are falling back. The whole force at camp turned out and fighting about one mile to left flank.'[12]

Actually Gardner has been premature, because the 'whole force' is not yet in action. But Cavaye, Mostyn and Dyson and their men are now falling slowly back towards the camp, keeping up their fire as they go as instructed by Essex. Essex turns and follows them, but his horse finds the rocky slope hard going and he has not gone far before the advance skirmishers of the uNokhenkhe Regiment appear on the rim of the escarpment above him and open fire. From below Colonel Pulleine can now see the leading warriors of the uKhandempemvu and uMbonambi coming over the rim of the plateau. They are advancing obliquely across his front to their right, and for an anxious moment it looks as if they might cut off the retreat of the companies on the spur.

12:20 p.m. Luckily the fire of the uNokhenkhe has so far been 'wild and ineffective',[13] and Essex reaches the bottom of the slope unscathed. Here he finds that Mostyn and Cavaye have brought their companies down in good order in time to avoid encirclement, and are busy deploying them into a firing line, facing north this time, with Captain Reginald Younghusband's C Company covering their left. What Essex cannot see is how few of Dyson's tiny detachment have made it back; the uNokhenkhe have caught up with them while still on top of the spur, and a number of red-coated bodies are scattered across the hill, out of sight of their comrades below.

Smith and Curling can now see large numbers of Zulus coming over the rim of the escarpment, and give the order to open fire with their 7-pounders.[14] As their shells burst among the massed enemy they see them open out into skirmish order and begin to spread out towards the flanks. But they continue to advance steadily, and soon their musket balls are falling among the gun crews and causing casualties.

Major Bengough and his men have crossed the Mzinyathi with the support of some of Beaumont's Border Guards and are now only about five miles as the crow flies from the field of battle. They halt to eat their midday meal among the rocks on the Zululand shore.[15] The African troops are eager for action and busy themselves with their pre-battle rituals. They can now hear artillery fire in the distance, but they have received no orders and have no idea what is happening in the hills to the north. Before he returns to his post on the Natal bank, William Beaumont informs Bengough that Lord Chelmsford has been planning a reconnaissance towards Mangeni, and the two officers agree that this is presumably the source of the firing. Bengough decides to stay where he is in the expectation that the general will send him further instructions;

perhaps he will be ordered to march to intercept any Zulus retreating in front of Chelmsford's advance. He does not realise that Chelmsford has no idea that he is there; orders have been issued for him to march to Rorke's Drift, and so his commanding officer presumes that that is where he is.

Lieutenant Scott's Carbineers are now forced to mount up and abandon their post on Amatutshane as the iNgobamakhosi sweep over it. Some of them manage to get through to join Durnford. He still has his mounted troopers under firm control and they are falling back in front of the advancing Zulus of the uVe and iNgobamakhosi in bounds of twenty to thirty yards, halting and dismounting after each brief retirement to shoot.[16] Every fourth man stays mounted, takes the other horses a few yards to the rear and holds their reins to prevent them from bolting until their owners have fired, run back to them and remounted.

Durnford knows that firing from horseback is too inaccurate to be worthwhile, and he is gambling that the delays imposed by having continually to mount and dismount will be offset by the fact that the enemy will be forced to go to ground by the more accurate volleys delivered on foot. They are inflicting casualties on the Zulus in front of them, but unfortunately the uVe and iNgobamakhosi are starting to outflank them on their right, and they do not have enough firepower to stop them.

Their colonel is a professional officer and has seen combat before, but the present situation is placing him under unprecedented strain. He is well aware that this is his opportunity to redeem his failure at Bushman's Pass, but already the opportunity is slipping away. Although he is the senior officer in the field, he has placed himself out on a flank where he cannot influence events where it matters. He can see – as Pulleine still cannot – that the right flank cannot be held in the long run, but he is too closely involved in the fighting there to be able to do more than delay the inevitable. Consequently he is in a state of extreme stress, and his subordinates notice that his orders do not always make sense.

Somewhere on the plain west of Amatutshane he encounters Private Johnson, the survivor of the rocket battery, and demands to know where his unit is. The battery has been overrun and Major Russell killed, Johnson tells him. Seeming not to understand, Durnford replies 'You had better go back and fetch him.'[17] The private points out that they are already almost surrounded by the Zulus, at which Durnford rides off and leaves him, alone and on foot. Johnson does not hesitate, but runs for his life. With his comrades, Grant and Trainer, he will be one of the few to succeed in escaping along the Rorke's Drift road before the Zulu right horn can spring its trap.

(Assuming that Johnson had been fleeing towards the camp and not away from it, at this point Durnford must have already encountered Captain Nourse, who had witnessed Russell's death and the loss of his battery. This makes the colonel's failure to grasp their fate even harder to understand. As we shall see, this was not the last time that he was heard enquiring about the whereabouts of the late major.)

12:25 p.m. Pulleine is making good progress in deploying a battalion-strength firing line at the foot of the escarpment. On his left he has C Company 1st/24th under Younghusband, then Mostyn's F and Cavaye's E Companies. On the right the guns are flanked by Degacher's A and Wardell's H Companies from the same battalion, with Pope's G Company 2nd/24th still trying to get into position on the far right. Various mounted volunteer detachments, and the NNC units of Captains Lonsdale and Krohn, are either prolonging the line on the flanks or slightly to the rear, having found what safety they can without masking the fire of the regulars. Pulleine is only too aware, however, that with no second line of regular infantry he will be in trouble if the enemy get round his flanks. Perhaps he has time to consider whether he can still pull the men back further into a battalion square which cannot be outflanked, and to regret the time lost in the failed attempt to reinforce the abandoned position on the spur.

For the moment, however, the defenders of the camp are holding their ground, and the prospects of victory seem good. Lord Chelmsford has been worrying about the possibility that the Zulus will avoid a major battle and withdraw their forces intact to fight a guerrilla campaign further along the road to oNdini. Clearly, now, this is not going to happen. Henry Curling will later record that 'None of us felt the least anxious as to the result.'[18]

The uKhandempemvu and uMbonambi regiments have been advancing at an angle to the British position as they follow Raw and Roberts's retiring horsemen, but they can now see the camp directly below them and are coming down the escarpment on either side of the notch, more or less directly towards the firing line. Meanwhile on their right the uNokhenkhe are descending the spur towards where Younghusband's and Mostyn's companies are waiting for them. The *izinduna* of the uKhandempemvu lead their men in the regiment's distinctive chant, recalling a past victory against the Xhosa, and dismissing the enemy's bullets as no more deadly than hailstones: '... we catch the rocks of the sky!' 'Catch! At the place of Hisi!' is the response.[19] But none of this bravado can be heard from the British firing line as it explodes into thunderous noise.

Major Smith and Lieutenant Curling fire shrapnel shells as fast as they can into the enemy masses. The effect of the first few rounds is dramatic, but the Zulus quickly observe that the crews have to step away from their pieces to avoid the recoiling carriages before they fire. Now, every time the guns prepare to shoot, the warriors throw themselves on the ground and let the shells pass over them. One spectacular direct hit is achieved on a small stone kraal that can be seen on the edge of the escarpment. Unfortunately, although Smith and Curling do not yet know it, their victims are a group of amaNgwane cavalry under Lieutenant Roberts, who have taken shelter there when they have been overtaken by the Zulus on their way back from their reconnaissance on the plateau. Roberts and several of his men meet their deaths in this friendly-fire incident.[20]

12:30 p.m. As the Zulus come within the effective range of the Martini Henry rifles – between 300 and 400 yards – their casualties start to mount. They are still too far away for their antiquated firearms to have much effect, and seeing their advantage the men of the 24th are calmly and confidently shooting them down. Captain Essex sees how the men near to him are 'laughing and chatting' as they reload and fire repeatedly, believing that they are 'giving the Zulus an awful hammering'.[21] Finally the attackers are driven to ground by the British fire, throwing themselves into the long grass or behind slight undulations in the ground to take advantage of every available scrap of cover.

George Hamilton Browne and his NNC battalion have made slow progress on their march back to the camp, and are still several miles away out on the plain to the east. Browne, aware now that something unusual is happening, takes up his field glasses and tries to make sense of the scene.[22] He sees the smoke of bursting shells, red-coated soldiers lying down and firing volleys, and 'a black shadow resting on the hills' which must be the chest of the Zulu army. Clearly a full-scale battle is in progress, but he concludes that the defenders are holding their ground. He quickly composes a message to Lord Chelmsford and sends a rider galloping back with it over the plain:

> The camp is being attacked on the left and in front and as yet
> is holding its own. Ground still good for the rapid advance of
> guns and horses. Am moving forward as fast as I can.

But, unseen by Essex, Curling and their companions, the three regiments of the Zulu right horn are even now beginning to outflank the British position, pouring down the escarpment wherever the terrain permits, with the objective of cutting the road to Rorke's Drift where it runs south of Isandlwana Hill. The uThulwana and the other regiments of the Undi corps, which form the loins of the army, are being led northwestward across the plateau to a position behind the right horn in case they are needed to reinforce it, but so far they have seen no fighting.[23]

The sound of firing is heard at Rorke's Drift. Several of the garrison are unhappy about being left out of the action and are impatient to know what is happening across the river in Zululand. Colour Sergeant Bourne takes a party of NCOs as far as the nearest crest of Shiyane

Hill which is visible from the post, but discovers that very little can be seen from there looking north or east.[24] What appears to be the top of the hill is in fact a false crest, and the real summit is roughly a mile further on, across a boulder-strewn plateau. Bourne cannot leave his post for the further hour it would take to get there and back, so he has to return. However, Surgeon Reynolds, the Reverend Otto Witt and George Smith, a local vicar serving as a temporary chaplain, have no urgent duties to attend to at the moment, and they decide to take a stroll to the top.

2:35 p.m. Durnford's men have now fallen back as far as the Nyogane donga, where they take up a defensive position. From here they can cover the far right of Pulleine's position, and Durnford orders a halt to further retirements. The horses are led into the donga where they are safe from Zulu fire. His troopers are joined by a selection of mounted men from various units, including some of Scott's Carbineers. Mehlokazulu kaSihayo, advancing with the iNgobamakhosi, sees the defenders deploying along the rim of the donga, which is so deep that only their helmets are visible.[25] There are several inches of water in the bottom, so that the men are wading in it up to their ankles. Only Durnford is still mounted, riding up and down the line controlling the fire of his troopers and occasionally stopping to help clear their jammed carbines. Unlike some of their NNC comrades, the mounted troops at least know how to set their sights, but they can still hardly be very expert with their weapons if an officer with one functional arm can do a better job of clearing stoppages.

Nevertheless, when they open fire the iNgobamakhosi directly in front of them find it impossible to advance in the open, and are forced either to take cover in the long grass or fall back over the ridge behind them. For the moment the Zulu left horn has been stopped. But on the other side of the field many of the uNokhenkhe, reaching the bottom of the spur, veer away to their right to escape the British fire and disappear around the western side of Isandlwana Hill, reinforcing the right horn.

12:45 p.m. Durnford realises that his men are running short of ammunition. His mounted contingent are the best-trained and most enthusiastic of all the African soldiers, but they are not accustomed to the fire discipline of the regulars, and they are expending their cartridges at a rapid rate. The colonel therefore sends Lieutenant Davies of the Edendale Troop back to the camp with fifteen men to collect more from Number Two Column's wagons.

Then Lieutenant Cochrane spots a large body of Zulus forming up around a cattle kraal to the left front, and asks Durnford whether he should send a messenger to ask the artillery to fire on them.[26] The colonel is worried that a request from a mere orderly might be ignored, so he tells Cochrane to go himself. The lieutenant gallops off in the direction of the camp.

1:00 p.m. The 1st/24th are also beginning to use up the rounds they have with them, and Edward Essex busies himself in organising a resupply. He enlists the help of the quartermaster of the 1st/24th, James Pullen, and some unemployed artillerymen, loads up a mule cart and sends it off to the front line, accompanied by men on foot carrying what they can.[27] Meanwhile an *induna* named Ndlaka, stationed somewhere on the slopes of Amatutshane, tries to encourage the stalled uMbonambi regiment to resume the attack by quoting Cetshwayo's order to 'Go and toss them into Maritzburg!'[28] Men start to rush forward, but Pope's G Company brings them under heavy fire and they soon go to ground again.

Reynolds, Witt and Smith reach the north-eastern end of the summit of Shiyane, and sit down on the rocks to take in the panoramic view. They can see for many miles into Zululand to the north and east, from the upper valley of the Mzinyathi River to the slopes of the Biggarsberg Mountains to the south. The only thing they cannot see is what is happening on the far side of Isandlwana, because the great bulk of the hill, some ten miles away, and the low ridges on either side, block their line of sight. They can still hear gunfire, however, so they stay where they are and continue to peer through their field glasses in the direction of the sound, hoping to gain some clue as to what must be happening over there.[29]

1:15 p.m. Lieutenant Davies has searched the camp in vain for the wagons carrying the desperately needed ammunition. He eventually finds a partly empty box with a few packets still in it and rides back towards the donga where Durnford is still holding out. The colonel is still feeling the strain, and one of his officers, Lieutenant Alfred Henderson, will later allege that he 'lost his head altogether; in fact I don't think he knew what to do'.[30] On the other hand his African troopers remain devoted to him; the Edendale man Jabez Molife will remember him as 'calm and cheerful'.[31] The officers of the uVe regiment on the Zulu far left are unaware of the ammunition situation in the donga and are reluctant to order another suicidal frontal charge, but they have been directing parties of their warriors still further to their left, under the cover of the low ridge that lies between them and Durnford's position. Now these Zulus realise that they are several hundred yards beyond the British right, effectively out of range of Durnford's troopers and with nothing but an open plain between them and the camp. The keen young Flycatchers get to their feet and run swiftly forward.

Durnford sees the outflanking warriors as they advance into the open, and in a split second he realises that the battle is lost. Even if he can somehow redeploy his men to defend their front and flank simultaneously, his ammunition resupply has still not arrived. He shouts the order to withdraw. The men mount and ride towards the camp, but their formations soon begin to disintegrate. The sudden change of fortune has unnerved many of them, and Durnford can no longer keep them under control. He is focusing on getting back to the vicinity of the camp and forming another defensive line, but the speed of his retreat looks to his men like flight, an example which they are quite happy to follow.

1:20 p.m. As Durnford falls back he inadvertently exposes the right flank of Lieutenant Pope's G Company, which is holding the far right of the regulars' firing line. Pope can only order the men on his right to wheel to the rear and try to face the enemy streaming past them, but he can do nothing to stop the envelopment of the camp. From his position in front of the camp Pulleine realises the extent of the disaster and orders a general retirement, with the intention of concentrating the defenders into rallying squares around the camp.[32]

At almost the same moment Ntshingwayo, watching from his command post on the top of the escarpment, decides that now is the time to make another attempt to advance in the centre. He turns to one of the *izinduna* accompanying him, Mkhosana kaMavundlana of the uKhandempemvu regiment, and orders him forward to rally his men and resume the advance. Mkhosana runs down to where his men are taking cover in the tall grass and, standing upright and conspicuous in his full dress regalia, reminds them of their king's commands. Their master 'gave no such order as this!' he shouts, gesturing at the prone warriors.[33] For a moment he seems immune to the British fire, and the uKhandempemvu rise to their feet and charge with a cry of '*Usuthu!*' The uMbonambi on their left rush forward again with them, and far away on the left the men of the iNgobamakhosi also see them go.

'There are the uKhandempemvu going into the tents!' shouts one of their *izinduna*,[34] and, eager to share the glory with their old rivals, the warriors surge forward in their turn. But as Mkhosana turns to join the charge a bullet strikes him in the head and he falls dead. His heroic action has had its desired effect, however. This time the attack is launched, not against a steady firing line, but against men who are beginning a difficult manoeuvre towards the rear, and perhaps are already starting to look over their shoulders towards their crumbling right flank.

1:25 p.m. The British NCOs bellow orders to their men to look to the front, but the Zulus cover the ground so fast that there is no time to form the separate companies into the shoulder to shoulder square that would give them their only chance of holding off such superior numbers for more than a few minutes. Instead they coalesce into a number of smaller squares, or rather clumps, as they withdraw towards the tents.

If we assume that each company could still muster around eighty men (which is probably an over-estimate), they would produce a square with at most twenty men on each side, covering a frontage of about ten paces if they were two deep and shoulder to shoulder. There is no room inside for officers, wounded or non-combatants, nor for ammunition boxes or men to hand out the cartridges. So these tiny 'squares' are not so much tactical solutions to the problem of encirclement as the last refuges of desperate men, seeking the support of their comrades in the hope of holding off the enemy for a few more moments. And once their ammunition supply begins to fail, and the Zulus can approach and throw spears from close range, the remaining infantrymen, too closely packed to dodge, will form a target which it is impossible to miss.

Major Smith's artillery pieces are suddenly left exposed as the infantry on either side of them fall back. They switch to firing canister, a form of ammunition which delivers a cloud of small lead bullets and can cut a swathe through enemy ranks at short range, but even this cannot stop the Zulus now. After a couple of rounds Smith orders the gunners to cease fire and limber up the guns.[35] But before they can do so, the enemy are upon them; several gunners are shot at close range, and one is actually stabbed to death as he is climbing onto the gun carriage. The major is hit in the arm by a musket ball, but he carries on commanding the retreat as his men jump onto the carriages and fall back towards the nek.

Lieutenant Cochrane has delivered his request for artillery support, but this has suddenly been overtaken by events. Now he is trying to rejoin Durnford, but cannot find him in the confusion. He decides that he has no choice but to make his escape.

Chelmsford receives Hamilton Browne's message, but is still not unduly worried. He is an experienced soldier, but unfortunately none of his experience has prepared him for this situation. The lesson he has learned from fighting the Xhosa is that African warriors cannot charge home against massed rifle fire from British regulars. If the Zulus are really initiating a full-scale battle, he is convinced that they will be beaten regardless of the relative numbers.

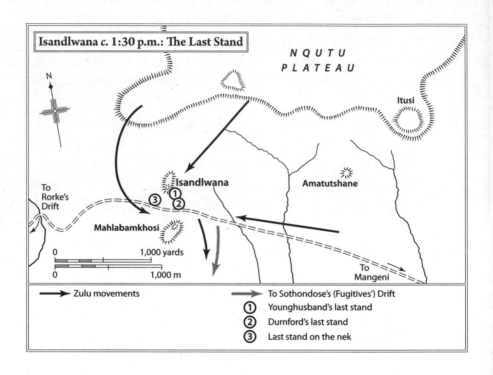

Isandlwana c. 1:30 p.m.: The Last Stand

NQUTU PLATEAU

Itusi

To Rorke's Drift

Isandlwana
① ②
③

Amatutshane

Mahlabamkhosi

0   1,000 yards
0   1,000 m

To Mangeni

→ Zulu movements
→ To Sothondose's (Fugitives') Drift
① Younghusband's last stand
② Durnford's last stand
③ Last stand on the nek

Looking north from the nek or saddle which lies between Isandlwana and
Mahlabamkhosi hills towards the Nqutu Plateau. The route of the British retreat
from the firing line is marked by a trail of burial cairns which indicate
the approximate positions where bodies were found after the battle. However,
it is not possible to link the burial sites reliably to the locations where men met
their deaths, as remains have been moved both during the initial burial process
and on various occasions since.

1:30 p.m. As the leading elements of the uNokhenkhe regiment emerge
from behind the hill and advance towards the wagons on the nek, the
encirclement of the camp is already virtually complete. Beyond them
the three regiments of the right horn are on the verge of cutting the
road to Rorke's Drift, although the hundreds of wagons and thousands
of frightened draught animals milling about on the nek are hampering
their advance.[36] Some of the fleeter-footed warriors are already racing
towards the valley of the Manzimnyama River, which flows about a

mile to the west of Isandlwana, running north to south towards its confluence with the Mzinyathi. Their *izinduna* have realised that, with their retreat to Rorke's Drift blocked, the British survivors will have to try to escape in this direction, and they are eager to make the encirclement complete.[37]

The companies of the 1st/24th continue to fall back towards the camp, and the British battle line breaks down into a series of isolated last stands. On horseback in the centre of the line Colonel Pulleine is a conspicuous figure, and as they come closer several of the uKhandempemvu and uMbonambi begin to concentrate their fire on him. His horse is killed under him and he falls heavily to the ground, but one of the company officers lends him another horse and he remounts.[38] As the Zulus rush forward towards the camp the colonel realises that his command is outflanked on both sides and is facing annihilation. He orders his adjutant, Lieutenant Melvill, to ride back to the camp, collect the Queen's Colour and take it to safety. For the flag to be captured by the Zulus would be the ultimate humiliation for the regiment.[39]

This is the last order that Pulleine is able to issue. The men of the uMbonambi Regiment are now so close that all he can do is steady the soldiers in his immediate vicinity as they try to form their square, defended by a hedge of bayonets facing in all directions. The uMbonambi will later receive recognition from their king as the first unit to enter the enemy camp. But the Zulus are reluctant to close with the formidable bayonets, whose reach is so much greater than their own stabbing assegais, so they throw spears from a distance hoping to create gaps in the British front.

Not all the British are heroes; Captain Essex notices that some of them are becoming 'unsteady', understandably so in the face of imminent destruction, and that their surviving officers are having to keep calling out to rally them and even have to remind them to fix their bayonets.[40]

Captain Nourse, as he gallops through the camp in search of an escape route, looks back and sees Pulleine amidst a group of fifty or so redcoats, stoically enduring the rain of missiles.[41] Most of the Zulus fire their muskets once as they begin their advance but then, rather than stop to reload, they drop them and resort to their throwing spears. These weapons have a range of around fifty paces; they seldom kill men outright, but rather wound and weaken them so that their formation is disrupted and they can be isolated and stabbed fatally at close quarters. But a few of the attackers still have loaded muskets, and one of them takes aim at the mounted officer who seems to be in command and brings him to the ground.

From six miles away Inspector George Mansel of the Mounted Police is scanning the camp through his field glasses.[42] He and forty-six of his troopers have been sent back by Lord Chelmsford, and have halted briefly on top of a ridge to try and make sense of what they can see ahead of them. Mansel notices some tents still standing, what appears to be powder smoke drifting away, and then the smoke and flash of artillery fire, but the distance is too great to reveal any more. Suddenly the camp, until now illuminated by bright sunshine, goes dark, 'as if a shadow [is] passing over it'. The guns do not fire again.

Mansel cannot be certain, but he suspects the grim truth – that what he has just seen is the movement of thousands of Zulus into the British camp. He does not know whether their attack has been successful or not. His men blithely assume that the firing has stopped because the Zulus have retired. Mansel is not so sure, though he does not yet appreciate that he has just witnessed the destruction of Pulleine and his entire force. 'It's all over now, sir,' remarks his sergeant, and Mansel replies 'Yes, and I hope it is the right way.'*

---

* Inspector Mansel's chronology appears to be confused, as he was allegedly ordered back towards the camp by Lord Chelmsford only after the receipt of Hamilton Browne's 1:30 message (see p. 80), which must have been sent at about this time. This means that he could not have been within sight of Isandlwana before 3 p.m. at the earliest. However, he can hardly have seen the guns in action after about 1:30. Here it is assumed that he had in fact left earlier, perhaps with the idea of accompanying Browne, although the two parties seem to have been unaware of each other at this stage.

The gunfire can be faintly heard as far away as Mangeni, where Chelmsford and his staff also turn their field glasses in the direction of Isandlwana. From this distance all they can see is the tents, with no signs of fighting or troop movements. Chelmsford rides down into the valley to supervise the construction of a new campsite to accommodate Pulleine's men when they arrive.[43]

At around the same time a Zulu named Mdlalose bursts into one of the tents looking for something to drink, and finds himself face to face with a British officer sitting at a table.[44] The officer draws a pistol and fires at him at close range; Mdlalose is hit in the cheek, but the wound, though painful, is not disabling, and he retaliates with a spear thrust. Leaving the dead man where he lies the Zulu staggers away. He is bleeding profusely and the wound will disfigure him for life, but he is triumphant. He believes that he has killed the British commander, the 'chief *induna* of the army', and in recognition of his feat he will be known ever afterwards by the name of Maqedindaba, 'He Who Finishes the Matter'.*

* Whether the officer whom Mdlalose killed was really Colonel Pulleine has been debated ever since. He gave no reason for his assumption that this was the 'chief *induna*', and most Zulus were unfamiliar with British rank insignia: in fact when Cetshwayo later chided his warriors for not bringing him any officer prisoners for interrogation, he was told that they could not tell the officers from the men. At this critical point in the battle the colonel's place was surely with his troops and not in his tent. It is of course possible that he had lost his nerve and retired to this temporary shelter, but we have the testimony of three other witnesses to exonerate him from this charge. Captain Nourse saw him in the middle of 'about half a company' of infantry, who were then killed with spears thrown from beyond the reach of their bayonets. However, Private Bickley later reported hearing Lieutenant Coghill telling Melvill that Pulleine had been shot, not speared. And George Hamilton Browne claimed to have discovered his body while riding across the battlefield on the following day. As Browne was on horseback it could hardly have been inside or under one of the tents, many of which were still standing after the battle. Colonel Snook argues that the spot where Browne saw the corpse must have been just outside the camp of the 2nd/24th, roughly in the centre of the line where the uMbonambi regiment first broke into the encampment. This would be

Others meet their ends in various ways. One man of the 24th is knifed in the back by a Zulu who has taken him unawares while he is defending himself against other opponents to his front.[45] Another soldier thrusts his bayonet through a Zulu's skull, but too late to prevent the man's assegai from embedding itself in his chest, so that both men fall to the ground locked together. A trooper of the Natal Mounted Police wrestles a warrior to the ground and kills him, but is himself stabbed to death before he can get up.*

By now, George Hamilton Browne is scanning the scene ahead at every opportunity to try and establish what his men are marching into. He can make out a 'dense swarm' of Zulus pouring into the camp, preceded by a 'huge mob of maddened cattle'. Unlike Inspector Mansel he realises at once the extent of the disaster that has taken place at Isandlwana. There is no chance now of linking up with the defenders as ordered, and even an immediate retreat across the exposed plain will be too dangerous. His only hope of survival is to avoid being spotted by the victorious enemy. He orders his battalion to fall back to a ridge in the rear.[46]

Browne then sends yet another report to Chelmsford, despatching Captain Develing with an oral message which he hopes will this time convey the urgency of the situation: 'For God's sake come back, the camp is surrounded and things I fear are going badly.' Browne then moves to the top of the ridge he has selected as a rallying point. He deploys his NNC companies into individual ring formations in Zulu style, and orders the white officers to dismount and hide themselves inside the rings, behind the black troops. From a distance his men now look like Zulus, and he can only hope that in this way they can escape detection.

---

a logical place for the commanding officer to be, and for the purpose of this reconstruction it is assumed that it was there that Pulleine met his death.

* The fates of these anonymous combatants have been reconstructed from Lieutenant-Colonel Wilsone Black's report on the bodies found during his visit to the battlefield in June 1879. From this evidence it is of course impossible to deduce a precise time of death, but the incidents can be taken as typical of many of the small unrecorded fights taking place around this time.

At around this time, anyone with the leisure to look around him might notice a strange darkening of the sky. A partial eclipse of the sun began to be visible in southern Africa around 1 p.m., but even at its height the light is only diminished by about 60 per cent, so that it never becomes completely dark. A warrior of the uNokhenkhe will later recall that, but for the fact that the sun was still visible high in the sky, he would have thought that they had been fighting until the evening, but the event is hardly noticed amidst the dust and smoke by most of the participants in the battle.[47]

1:35 p.m. Durnford reaches the nek and looks around for his men, but as far as most of them are concerned the battle is already lost, and they have simply kept riding in the direction of Rorke's Drift or the Mzinyathi River. He sees Edward Essex, who is himself making his escape, and asks him to collect some men to help him make another stand. Essex can see that everyone in the vicinity is either fully occupied or running for their lives, so he soon gives this up as a bad job and keeps going.[48] Durnford may not have distinguished himself as a tactician, but he does not lack courage. Instead of escaping himself he rides on towards the camp, and on the way joins up once more with Captain Nourse, who is fleeing in the opposite direction. He asks again where Major Russell and his battery are, as if he cannot take in, or has already forgotten, what Nourse and Private Johnson have told him. When the captain confirms their fate Durnford is visibly upset but seems preoccupied with his own prospects, remarking only that he will not survive the disgrace.[49]

1:40 p.m. Finally Durnford manages to gather together a few men who are still prepared to fight: they include the remnants of the Natal Carbineers who have fought their way back from Amatutshane, and a few dozen soldiers from the 24th who have been collected by Quartermaster Pullen. With them he makes a stand on the eastern side of the nek, between the camp and the hill of Mahlabamkhosi to the south.

The two horns of the Zulu *impi* finally converge on the nek half a mile west of Durnford's position, 'where the old Dutch road used to

The view south-east down the valley of the Mzinyathi River – just visible at the extreme left – from near the Melvill and Coghill grave site. Five miles away in this direction, while their comrades were being done to death around Isandlwana, Major Bengough's NNC battalion sat and waited for orders which never came.

go across' in the words of Mehlokazulu.[50] But the last large formed body of British infantry has made it this far and chooses to make a stand here.[51] The square is gradually overwhelmed like the others, but under the cover of its fire some of the mounted fugitives are still getting through along the road which leads to Rorke's Drift. Among them are Henderson's Tlokoa and Charlie Raw with his troop of Zikhali's Horse from Durnford's command.

The Edendale men, however, have missed their chance of following along this route. In the confusion of the retreat from the Nyogane donga they have lost sight of their officer, Lieutenant Davies, but have been rallied by their sergeant, Simeon Nkambule. He is a highly respected member of the Edendale community, whose father Elijah has also served the British with distinction; he was Durnford's interpreter and was killed beside him at Bushman's Pass. Nkambule tells the men that their lives depend on keeping together, and that any man who leaves the ranks will die, but if they obey him, God willing, he will get them safely back to Natal.[52]

However, he realises that they are very short of ammunition, so he rides up to one of the 24th's wagons, which the Zulus have not yet reached, in search of more. He finds a young drummer sitting on the wagon and asks him for some cartridges, but the lad refuses, explaining that the ammunition belongs to the infantry and that he has orders to look after it. In what is an extraordinarily civilised exchange in the circumstances, Nkambule accepts his decision but, pointing out that the battle is lost, he offers to take the youth to safety with him on his horse. This, too, is refused, the drummer replying that he has been put there by his officer and he cannot desert his post. Nkambule and his men content themselves with collecting as many cartridges as they can from those which have been left scattered in the grass by the soldiers in their haste, then they reluctantly ride away and leave the boy to his fate.*

The two guns belonging to Smith and Curling also find their way along the road blocked. The two officers briefly confer with Nevill Coghill, Colonel Glyn's orderly, whom they encounter on the nek, about the possibility of making a stand there, but Coghill advises them that it cannot be done. Coghill in fact has been left in camp with an injured knee and is more or less *hors de combat*, although he can still ride. In any case the gun teams have not waited for them, but are already

---

* The Rev. Owen Watkins's account, based on Simeon Nkambule's reminiscences, refers to a 'little drummer boy', but we should not imagine that he was a child. The youngest drummer recorded as being at Isandlwana was eighteen, and most were in their twenties. This makes Simeon's offer to take the 'boy' onto his horse even more unselfish, since the extra weight would have slowed them down dangerously.

The memorial to the dead of the 24th Foot at Isandlwana.

The Mzinyathi River, looking upstream from the modern road crossing at Rorke's Drift. The ferries, or 'ponts', were moored in this relatively wide, slow-flowing stretch, and it was here that the British infantrymen were ferried over the river on 11 January.

The distinctive peak of Isandlwana (on the skyline just left of centre), seen from the Natal side of the Mzinyathi River at Rorke's Drift, where Lord Chelmsford's column crossed into Zululand on 11 January 1879. Although not visible from the Rorke's Drift mission station itself owing to the intervening Shiyane Hill – the lower slopes of which can be seen here on the right – Isandlwana can be clearly seen from the crossing, from where it reminded the men of the 24th Foot of the sphinx featured on their cap badge.

A view of the Isandlwana battlefield from near the modern mission station, which is located north of the hill itself near the base of the escarpment which marks the edge of the Nqutu Plateau. Amatutshane Hill (known to the British as the 'Conical Koppie') is visible at centre left, and in the distance can be seen the hills around Mangeni where Major Dartnell made contact with the Zulus on 21 January. Inclement weather conditions such as those seen here are not unusual in January, although the day of the battle itself was hot and sunny.

Looking south from the edge of the Nqutu Plateau towards
Isandlwana Hill and the valley of the Mzinyathi beyond. This
is the view that the warriors of the uKhandempemvu regiment
would have had as they came over the escarpment about noon
on 22 January, although there were no buildings in this area in
1879. The low rocky ridge behind which the British infantry
deployed can be seen running from left to right on the far side
of the road. The white dots to the left of Isandlwana, beneath the
rise known as Mahlabamkhosi, are the cairns that mark the last
resting places of British and colonial soldiers in the region of the
last stand on the nek. The fugitives' route to Sothondose's Drift
after the battle ran behind Mahlabamkhosi and towards the far
left of the picture.

The hill of Amatutshane seen from the site of the modern mission station. Durnford's position in the Nyogane donga extended to the right of Amatutshane, and the iNgobamakhosi and uVe regiments advanced behind the feature from left to right to outflank him. Meanwhile the warriors of the uMbonambi and uKhandempemvu were moving in the same direction in front of the hill towards the British camp.

Seen from the vicinity of the camp looking east, the Nyogane donga in which Durnford's men made their stand runs behind and to the right of the group of buildings in the left foreground. The plain in front of the donga is less flat than it appears; the low ridge in the middle distance enabled the warriors of the uVe regiment to extend their line under cover until they were able to outflank the position further to the right.

A group of cairns situated about 200 yards south-east of Isandlwana commemorates a number of colonial as well as British soldiers, and is often identified as the probable site of Anthony Durnford's last stand. The observer is struck immediately by the lack of cover in this part of the battlefield, or of anywhere – apart from the hill itself – where the defenders could have taken advantage of difficult ground to delay the Zulu onslaught. Here they stood at bay, and were killed, in ad hoc groups wherever they were overtaken.

Rorke's Drift, and here at Isandlwana, are the only places in the country where the South African and British flags fly side by side in memory of the men of both sides who fought and died here.

The Fugitives' Trail leading down to Sothondose's Drift, seen from the Natal side of the Mzinyathi River. Isandlwana Hill is approximately four miles away, beyond the high ground in the distance. Most of those escaping from the battlefield probably came over the hill on the horizon or the lower ridge to its left. The river itself is out of sight from here at the bottom of the gorge.

Typical hillside vegetation on the north slope of Shiyane Hill overlooking Rorke's Drift. It is down this slope that Otto Witt would have us believe that he rode his horse at speed. While the more level areas in the region are – and were in 1879 – largely grassy and easy to traverse, the rocky hills and escarpments are often covered with these spiny aloes, which although seldom mentioned in accounts of the fighting must have slowed down the movements of formed bodies of troops considerably.

The view from the top of Shiyane Hill towards Isandlwana, which is visible on the skyline in the centre at a distance of about ten miles. From this vantage point Otto Witt, George Smith and James Reynolds could observe Prince Dabulamanzi's army advancing across the plain and descending into the Mzinyathi Valley to the right in the hour or so after 2 p.m., but the events in and around the camp were concealed by Isandlwana Hill and the raised neks, or saddles, on either side. Consequently the watchers at first supposed that what they could see were victorious British troops returning from the battlefield.

The rocky ridge on the slope of Shiyane Hill, overlooking the Rorke's Drift post. The small bell tower on the skyline at centre right is remembered in local tradition as marking the place where Prince Dabulamanzi stood in the early stages of the fighting.

Left: Taken from the same spot as the photograph at top left, with a zoom lens at approximately thirty times magnification, this picture confirms the impossibility of seeing anything of the fighting, even with a telescope, at Isandlwana from the neighbourhood of Rorke's Drift – Isandlwana Hill blocks the line of sight..

Above: The Rorke's Drift mission station seen from Shiyane Hill, looking north into Zululand. The modern museum – formerly the hospital – is on the left and the church, which served as a storehouse during the battle, is on the right. The larger building in the foreground and the trees which now partially obscure the lines of sight were not there in 1879. Beyond the post, the road to the drift, the Batshe Valley and Isandlwana winds into the distance.

Top right: The site of the museum/hospital at Rorke's Drift, seen from the north-west. The men of the Zulu iNdluyengwe regiment veered to the left after their initial assault against the other side of the perimeter was checked and deployed near this spot, extending their line to the left. Although the modern buildings were erected after the battle, and are roofed with iron rather than thatch, they are built on the same foundations as the originals and their dimensions and style are very similar.

Right: This surviving section of the rocky 'step' which ran along the north side of the perimeter at Rorke's Drift, with the church/storehouse in the background, may give some idea of the difficulties which the attacking Zulus faced here. When topped with mealie bags and determined infantrymen with fixed bayonets, the position would have taken a fit and agile man as well as a brave one to storm.

The memorial to the British defenders at Rorke's Drift. The names of the dead were added shortly after the battle by Bandsman Melsop, who in civilian life had been a stonemason. He was said to have employed his bayonet for the job as he lacked the proper tools, but this seems improbable in view of the high quality of the carving.

driving recklessly down the steep rocky slope to the left which leads to the valley of the Manzimnyama River.[53] Their wild career can only end one way, and a hundred yards down the hill the guns and teams crash into an unseen donga; the guns are overturned and the drivers thrown to the ground. As Coghill, Smith and Curling gallop by they see Zulus already in amongst them, stabbing the men and horses to death. Just behind them Surgeon-Major Shepherd has managed to load a group of wounded men onto an ambulance wagon, sending it off towards the nek and telling Band Sergeant Gamble and his bandsmen, who double as stretcher bearers in battle, to look after themselves. But with the road firmly closed, and the only other way out down the hill, the wagon has to be abandoned. None of the wounded will be seen alive again.

1:45 p.m. The Zulus of the right horn are now in force across the escape route over the nek, forcing the men still fleeing from the battlefield to swing to their left and risk a dash to the Mzinyathi River. Some of the local men in the NNC know of a crossing, named Sothondose's Drift after a local chief, which although difficult and dangerous at this time of year, with the river in flood, might at least give them a chance of reaching Natal. There is no marked path, and the fugitives will need first to follow the guns into the valley of the Manzimnyama River, which flows north to south about two miles west of the nek, cross the stream and then climb over the shoulder of Mpethe Hill, before beginning the rocky descent to the Mzinyathi. The total distance is about four miles, and in places it is too steep to ride safely, but these men are running for their lives.

Simeon Nkambule looks ahead and sees Anthony Durnford waving his good arm and shouting as he rallies the men with him into a rough square. Behind him the Zulus are now swarming across the road to Rorke's Drift, so the Edendale men swing their horses around and start for Sothondose's Drift without further delay.[54]

Durnford and his little band have been fighting off hundreds of encircling Zulus, for a few moments at least preventing the iNgobamakhosi and uVe from breaking into the camp from the east.

Once the ammunition for their carbines is expended they throw them to the ground and resort to their revolvers. Mehlokazulu of the iNgobamakhosi is among the men closing in on them amid the smoke and the dust, and at the last he sees them draw their knives and form up close together in a line for mutual support.[55] This is no more than a defiant gesture, and they are soon overwhelmed by the missiles and stabbing spears of their opponents. From a distance Harry Davies spots his colonel standing surrounded by Zulus, his orderly trying to protect him with a drawn sword. When it is all over Mehlokazulu looks down at the bodies and notes among them one particular officer lying in the midst of the dead Carbineers and others, 'with his arm in a sling and a big moustache'. Anthony Durnford has made his last stand.

George Shepstone has also somehow become separated from the rest of Durnford's command and is rallying his own group of men for a stand further west, among the rocks on the south-western side of Isandlwana. They include many of the isiGqoza, Cetshwayo's old enemies, who unlike most of their comrades in the NNC are reluctant to run from the Zulus. They are surrounded by the uNokhenkhe and fight to the death. Shepstone himself, as Zulu witnesses will later recall, displays great courage and kills many of his opponents. But like all the other little bands, his men fall one by one under the hail of missiles.[56]

1:50 p.m. A man named Umtweni rushes in and stabs George Shepstone to death while he is reloading. Within minutes the rest of his force is wiped out.

Now the way is open to the camp from all directions and the Zulus advance at a steady walk, breaking into a run for the last 150 yards. James Brickhill hears them give a triumphant cry, '*Luminyile Elsutu!*' He is a fluent Zulu speaker and understands it all too well: 'The Usuthu have overwhelmed!'[57] Brickhill rides back to the camp to see if he can find Quartermaster Pullen, but without success; Pullen is already lying dead in the vicinity of Durnford's stand, having led a small group of men in a suicidal bid to stop the iNgobamakhosi turning the right flank.[58] Seeing that the camp is lost, Brickhill turns his horse and

The nek beneath Isandlwana Hill, where the British wagon train was parked before the battle. On the right is the memorial to the dead of the 24th Foot, marking roughly the location of the last stand on this part of the field.

gallops towards the nek. Behind him Troopers Sparks and Pearce of the Mounted Police also prepare to mount up and flee, but Pearce has left his horse's bit in his tent. Sparks urges him to leave it or they will be killed, but his comrade turns back, muttering something about how the sergeant-major will tell him off if he sees him riding with an improvised snaffle instead of the regulation metal bit. Sparks rides on, but the Zulus are coming up to surround the tent and Trooper Pearce is never seen again.[59] Another of the last fugitives, galloping away, sees an unknown British officer and a Zulu facing each other in a man-to-man duel. The officer has emptied his revolver into the enemies in front of him, then drawn his sword and put his back against the wheel of a wagon. The Zulu advances towards him, dodging from side to side and moving his shield in front of him to protect himself. Then he suddenly lowers the shield, and the officer strikes with his sword at his head. But the manoeuvre is a trick; the warrior lifts his shield again, and the sword bites into it and becomes stuck. A quick twist of the shield pulls the sword from the unwary officer's grasp, and now that he is unarmed a spear thrust finishes him.[60]

Captain Nourse has lost his horse and run out of bullets for his revolver; he almost gives himself up for dead and is looking for a convenient donga to make a last stand, when his African groom appears out of nowhere, mounted and leading the captain's horse. The groom does not wait to discuss the situation, but immediately gallops away; nevertheless, Nourse is now mounted, and what is more he finds a loaded revolver attached to the saddle. He rides into the herd of thousands of frightened horses, mules, cattle and sheep on the nek, and somehow in the dust and noise the Zulus do not spot him.[61]

For a few minutes the route to Sothondose's Drift has been uncontested by the Zulus, but that window of opportunity has now passed. Those who are embarking on the descent from now on are forced to run the gauntlet of groups of warriors who have hurried ahead to cut them off. However, it is now easier for those unfamiliar with the country to follow the route, marked as it is by a trail of discarded equipment. As a transport officer Horace Smith-Dorrien can do no more in the camp, and he has access to a good horse.[62] Following the trail at speed he passes the two artillery pieces overturned in the donga and being looted by the Zulus. Soon afterwards he overtakes their officer, Lieutenant Curling, who has lost his companions and seems to be unsure of what to do; Smith-Dorrien urges him to keep moving. James Brickhill travels in a bunch of men, mules, horses and oxen all mixed up together, picking their way over the discarded guns, spears, shields and clothing which are scattered over the hillside. He encounters Band Sergeant Gamble staggering amongst the rocks, on foot and helpless. Gamble pleads with him; 'For God's sake give me a lift,' but Brickhill closes his eyes and rides on, muttering 'My dear fellow, it's a case of life and death with me.' A little further on he passes another soldier on foot, too exhausted to continue, who sits down on a rock and tells him 'The Zulus can just come up and stab me if they like.' As far as Brickhill will ever know, they do just that.[63]

Chapter 5

Afternoon

'Their deaths could not have been more noble.'
(Richard Glyn, London Gazette, *April 1879)*

2:00 p.m. George Hamilton Browne sees a group of mounted men appear in the distance on the plain behind him and halt. He assumes that they have been sent in response to Captain Develing's message and sends another officer across to ask them to hurry up. In fact Develing is only now approaching the position at Mangeni.[1] The first people he encounters are F and H Companies of the 2nd/24th, under Captains Church and Harvey, and Colonel Harness with the four guns which have been following Chelmsford. They have been left far in the rear of the commander-in-chief's advance to Mangeni, and have halted on a rise while Major Wilsone Black tries to locate Chelmsford and find out where they are to go. They are puzzled by the sight of what appears to be a force of Zulus several hundred strong on the plain to the west. (In fact the Zulu left horn is several miles closer to Isandlwana, and this must be Browne and his NNC, who have somehow passed them without being seen.) At this point Black returns, accompanied by one of Chelmsford's ADCs, a Major Gossett. Develing passes on the message from Browne and, although Gossett is sceptical, Colonel Harness decides to turn around and march to assist Browne's beleaguered battalion. Gossett returns to Mangeni to report to the general.

The victorious Zulus are now looting the British camp. They destroy the tents and the food, fearing that it might have been poisoned. They are less discriminating about drink, as they are all desperately thirsty after hours of fighting in the hot sun, and some of them swig from bottles of ink or paraffin in their search for beer. They kill the horses, which they know will be valuable to the white men if they manage to recapture them, but they drive off the oxen as booty. They have not seen mules before and Cetshwayo has given no orders concerning them, so they generally leave them alone. Most of the officers' pet dogs, attempting to guard their masters' tents, are quickly despatched in the frenzy. The warriors take any rifles and other weapons they can find, as well as watches and similar valuables.[2] Zofikasho Zungu is one of many who pick up red coats and officers' braided headgear as souvenirs. Ironically, in view of the claims which will later be made about the role of ammunition shortages in the British defeat, they find thousands of cartridges in the wagons, and have no difficulty in getting into the boxes; according to Mehlokazulu they smash them open with stones picked up on the battlefield. The Martini Henry cartridges do not fit the Zulus' muskets, but they can extract the bullets and pour out the loose gunpowder inside.

The treatment of the British dead will later cause a great deal of bad feeling, as the corpses are repeatedly stabbed even after death, then their abdomens are ripped open with spear blades. In fact, although the victims' comrades do not at first understand this, their treatment is more a mark of respect than of brutality. When hunting lions the Zulus traditionally allow three men to stab the beast and share in the honour of killing it – a custom known as '*hlomula*'. By doing this now they are according the redcoats the same status as a quarry as the lions, which is a tribute to their courage and fighting ability. The cutting open of the bodies, or '*qaqa*', is done to free the spirits of the dead and prevent them from remaining on earth to haunt their killers.[3]

The four regiments of the Zulu reserve have not been committed to the battle at Isandlwana in time to draw blood, and now find themselves far away from the action on the right wing. The senior among them is the uThulwana, Cetshwayo's own unit and the equivalent in the Zulu army of a guard regiment. They are named in honour of a Sotho chief, Thulare, but their alternative title, the amaBoza, refers to the dust they raise as they drive off enemy cattle. Formed around 1850, the regiment consists of men around fifty years of age, many of them veterans of

Cetshwayo's great victory at Ndondakusuka in 1856. The men of the associated iNdlondlo or 'Crested mamba' regiment are two or three years younger, but share their veteran status, as do those of the uDloko, or 'Young crested mamba', who are in their mid-forties. Brigaded with them are the younger men of the iNdluyengwe regiment, named after the spotted coat of the leopard, who were born around 1847 and so are now in their early thirties and newly married. All these senior warriors carry predominantly white shields and wear the head ring that denotes married warriors. They regard themselves as superior to the youngsters who have seen all the action so far, and are unhappy about missing their chance for loot and glory.

Voices are raised, demanding to be led against the enemy. They know that there are redcoats at kwaJimu, as they call the Rorke's Drift station, guarding the stores of food and gunpowder. Their *izinduna*, fearful of losing control, look expectantly towards Prince Dabulamanzi. The prince does not hold a formal command, but as the king's brother he is the highest-ranking Zulu present. He hesitates briefly – he knows that Cetshwayo has forbidden his troops to cross into Natal – but the men are determined not to be deprived of the rewards of battle which their comrades have already achieved. As the clamour grows, Dabulamanzi realises that his options are either to lead the attack or be accused of losing control of the men. Reluctantly, he signals the advance towards Rorke's Drift.[4] The younger and swifter footed iNdluyengwe are to descend to the Mzinyathi River and cross at a narrow gorge about a mile upstream of Sothondose's Drift, then advance along the Natal bank and round the southern flank of Shiyane Hill. Part of the regiment will follow Zibhebhu kaMaphitha, split off from the left flank and reinforce the men of the right horn who are still fighting to close off the escape route to Sothondose's Drift. Meanwhile the older men will take a more direct route to cross the river east of Shiyane Hill, approximately two miles downstream of the British post.

From on top of Shiyane, Reynolds, Witt and Smith can see large bodies of men moving on their side of Isandlwana Hill, and at first imagine them to be their own NNC troops. But then they begin to

The Mzinyathi River at Sothondose's Drift, looking upstream from the Natal bank with Zululand on the right. It was somewhere near here that Melvill, Coghill and the other fugitives crossed the Mzinyathi just after 2 p.m. This picture was taken in October, during the dry season; in January 1879 the river was much higher and faster-flowing.

notice horsemen, individually and in small groups, galloping wildly in their direction. The first doubts about the outcome of the unseen battle begin to grow in their minds. Surgeon Reynolds is worried that there might have been unexpectedly heavy casualties, and that the riders might be messengers coming for medical assistance. He hurries back towards the post, leaving Witt and Smith to follow on behind.[5]

Along what will become known as the Fugitives' Trail to Sothondose's Drift, the rout and the slaughter continue. Some of the fugitives' escapes are little short of miraculous. Horace Smith-Dorrien notes that the Zulus are more infuriated with the African soldiers and drivers than they are with the whites, perhaps regarding them as traitors, and seem to concentrate on killing them first. He also sees that all the white officers who get away are wearing dark blue patrol jackets instead of red coats, and later he will wonder whether the enemy are taking literally their king's order to kill the '*amasoja ebomvu*' or 'redcoat soldiers'.[6] Trooper Dorehill, of the Mounted Police, has reached the Mzinyathi and is looking for a place to cross when he sees two young Zulus running towards him, followed by an older married man wearing a head ring.[7] As he prepares to jump into the raging river he hears two shots behind him. Supposing that the Zulus have fired at him and missed, he glances back to see the older man standing over the bodies of the other two warriors with a smoking double-barrelled shotgun. 'Jump into the river!' the man shouts in isiZulu. Dorehill does so, and manages to get across by holding on to the tail of his horse. On the far side he meets two other fugitives, Sergeant Costello of the Royal Artillery and a Mounted Infantryman, Private Gascoigne. Costello has got away on a splendid black horse belonging to his officer, Major Smith.

The three men are suddenly distracted by the cries of Trooper Hayes, who has been sharing a tent with Dorehill. Last night Hayes had a premonition of disaster and disturbed his companion's sleep with his nightmares. Now he has got across the Mzinyathi only to become stuck in the mud on the far side and have his horse stolen by another fugitive. They pull Hayes out, then Gascoigne – who must be a better rider than most of the Mounted Infantry – catches up with the horse thief, knocks him off the animal's back and reunites it with Hayes. Meanwhile, about twenty Zulus have appeared on the far bank and opened fire, and there is no sign of Dorehill's mysterious rescuer. The three men ride off unscathed, although Costello is saved only by Major Smith's riding cloak, which is still rolled up on the back of the saddle and is struck by several musket balls.

Smith-Dorrien is still on his way over the summit of Mpethe Hill when Lieutenant Melvill overtakes him carrying the Queen's Colour.

James Hamer, a civilian on Durnford's staff, has managed to get as far as the Manzimnyama Ravine before his horse stops, too tired to go on. Just at that moment a man from the rocket battery rides up leading a spare horse and hands the reins to Hamer. He quickly takes the saddle off his blown horse and mounts up, just as a group of Zulus behind them fire a volley. Both Hamer's old horse and his rescuer are shot dead, but Hamer rides off unhurt.[8]

The Edendale men's officer, Harry Davies, has to fight his way through the enemy on several occasions.[9] Six hundred yards from the camp he and a Carbineer who is with him come upon two Zulus stabbing a couple of soldiers to death, and shoot them both with their revolvers. Davies's horse has been speared in the leg while crossing the nek, and eventually it falters and he has to dismount and lead it while it recovers its strength. Two more Zulus see him slow down and so they rush towards him; he tries to ward them off with his rifle and fixed bayonet, but one Zulu snatches the weapon out of his hand and grabs his horse's bridle. Davies is staring death in the face when his startled horse rears and kicks out, forcing the Zulu to step back. The other warrior throws a spear but misses, and Davies manages to draw his revolver and dispatch them both. As he mounts up again and rides on he sees yet more Zulus appear ahead of him, but once again his skill with a pistol saves his life; as he gallops towards them he takes aim at the man directly in front of him and shoots him in the head. The other Zulus jump aside and Davies charges through them. Luckily he is as good a horseman as he is a pistol shot, and when he reaches the Mzinyathi he swims his horse across holding on to a stirrup.*

* The revolver was difficult to shoot accurately and lacked stopping power at anything beyond point-blank range, and was generally regarded as of little use in military operations except, as the explorer Harry Johnston put it, 'for accidentally shooting oneself'. However, at Isandlwana, especially in the pursuit phase, it came into its own. It could be fired with one hand from horseback and, unlike the rifles of the day, it could discharge several shots in rapid succession, making it ideal for use against numerous opponents at very close range. At this period officers were not issued with sidearms but had to purchase them privately, so there was a wide variety

The rest of the Edendale troop under Simeon Nkambule are the only unit to have retained any sort of order during the retreat towards the river, and now that the battle is won the Zulus are reluctant to risk attacking them when there are so many easier targets available. When they reach the Mzinyathi the troopers halt for a few moments to give covering fire to the mob of fugitives converging on Sothondose's Drift. Then they plunge into the water, driving all the oxen and riderless horses that they can find in front of them, and calling out for the dismounted fugitives in the vicinity to hold on to their stirrups. On the Natal bank they halt and turn again. Lieutenant Erskine of the 1st NNC is scrambling out of the water when he hears the Edendale men shouting at him to lie flat on his horse's neck. He does so and they fire a volley over his head, cutting down several Zulus on the opposite bank who are about to shoot at him. Then Sergeant Nkambule leads his men up the hill and away in the direction of Helpmekaar.[10]

Twenty-two-year-old Private Samuel Wassall of the Mounted Infantry reaches the river still on horseback, only to see one of his comrades, Private Westwood, being swept downstream. He hastily tethers his Basuto pony to a tree, dives into the rushing water and manages to drag Westwood back to the shore. Luckily Wassall's horse is still there, and he pulls his companion up behind him and together they get across to the Natal bank, despite heavy but inaccurate fire from a party of Zulus who appear behind them. Wassall's heroic feat has been seen by Captain William Barton of Zikhali's Horse, and he will later become the only survivor of Isandlwana to receive the Victoria Cross.[11] For a moment now he considers retreating to Rorke's Drift, but he realises that the Zulus are likely to be converging on the post in

---

of models in use. The most popular was probably the six-shot .45 calibre Adams Mark III, which had the important advantage that it was double-action; in other words it could be cocked and fired with a single pull of the trigger rather than having to cock the hammer after each shot. This required a slightly harder pull than single-action weapons such as the Colt, and made the aim rather more erratic, but in life or death situations at close quarters this was more than compensated for by the speed with which successive shots could be fired.

the aftermath of their victory, so instead he sets off on his sturdy little pony in the direction of Helpmekaar.

As Horace Smith-Dorrien reaches the Mzinyathi he sees a wounded mounted infantryman lying among the boulders and stops to bandage his bleeding arm. As he does so he hears someone shout 'Get on man; the Zulus are on top of you!' and looking back he sees Major Smith coming towards him, almost surrounded by Zulus. Smith-Dorrien draws his revolver and somehow manages to shoot his way out, but he sees Major Smith killed, and has his own horse speared before, dismounted, he jumps off a steep bank and straight into deep water. Henry Curling also sees Smith die as he steers his horse down the bank and into the river. Curling gets over safely with three or four men clinging on to his horse's tail and stirrup leathers.

Meanwhile, Smith-Dorrien faces imminent drowning without the aid of his horse, but he manages to grab the tail of a stray animal as it swims past, and it pulls him across. Once he is on the shore, however, he is too tired to remount and the horse gets away. He has no choice but to run up the hill on foot, soaking wet, being knocked over several times by mounted fugitives rushing past. He sees about twenty Zulus cross after him, but they have not managed to bring their guns over the river and are too far away to catch him. Then he comes across James Hamer, who has been kicked by his horse and is too badly hurt to mount unaided. Smith-Dorrien stops to help him onto the horse and even lends him his knife. Hamer promises to catch another horse and bring it back for his rescuer, but Smith-Dorrien does not see him again.[12]

2:10 p.m. Lieutenant Walter Higginson reaches Sothondose's Drift to find Melvill, Coghill and Cochrane about to cross together.[13] Higginson rides his horse into the water, but when it stumbles he falls off and is swept downstream. He manages to hold on to a large rock, and sees Melvill also in the water, having lost his grip on the colour as he fell. Higginson grabs the flag as it drifts past him, but the force of the water pulls him off the rock and he has to let it go again. Meanwhile,

A cairn of stones near the Melvill and Coghill grave site, erected over the body of a Zulu 'unknown soldier'. The precise identity of the Zulus who took up the pursuit of the fugitives on the Natal side of the river remains uncertain.

Coghill has got across to the far bank, but on seeing his friends' plight he rides back to help. The Zulus on their side of the river see him and open fire, killing his horse, so that all three officers are now floundering in the water. Melvill manages to seize the colour again, but as they struggle to the shore the current finally snatches it from his hand and sweeps it away.*

* This is one of the few timings that can be independently corroborated. Three months later Colonel Glyn retrieved Melvill's gold watch from his body, and

Edward Essex, Alan Gardner, William Cochrane and Walter Stafford meet up on the Natal bank and realise that there is no one else coming behind them. It appears that the fugitives from Isandlwana have all either crossed the river already or been killed. Gardner writes a brief note and gives it to a mounted infantryman to take to Rorke's Drift, warning the garrison that the Zulus are on their way in force.[14] Then they make their way up the hill towards Helpmekaar.

2:15 p.m. As they pick their way on foot up the steep rocky slope on the far side of the Mzinyathi, the injured Coghill now having to be almost dragged by his comrades, Melvill and Higginson breathe a sigh of relief. Looking back, they can see that most of the Zulus do not seem to be trying to cross the swollen river in pursuit, and the few who do get across are quickly being recalled by their *izinduna*, conscious of the king's instructions not to invade Natal. But they are not safe yet. Some of the local Nxumalo people have gathered on the Natal side to watch the unfolding drama, and the pursuers call to them across the river, urging them to turn on the white soldiers or risk the wrath of a victorious Cetshwayo. 'If you don't kill them we will kill you!' one of them shouts.

Suddenly Coghill catches sight of two Zulus running up behind them, and shouts 'Here they come!' Higginson, who is unarmed, replies, 'For God's sake fire,' and Melvill and Coghill draw their revolvers and shoot both men down. The effort seems to exhaust them finally, and they tell Higginson that they can go no further. Even if Melvill still has the strength to continue, that would mean leaving his helpless friend behind, which would be unthinkable. Higginson leaves them in the shelter of a boulder and runs on.[15]

2:20 p.m. Some time in the next few minutes a party of warriors stumbles across Melvill and Coghill slumped beside the boulder. The two officers are ready for them and shoot several more of their assailants, whose

---

found that water had got into the mechanism and stopped it at ten minutes past two. This, he concluded, 'must have been about the time they crossed the Buffalo'.

This memorial to Lieutenants Melvill and Coghill was later erected close to where their bodies were discovered, high above the river on the Natal side, where they must have at least briefly thought themselves safe from further pursuit.

bodies are later found with theirs as a testimony to the violence of the struggle, but they are soon overwhelmed and speared to death. None of their friends sees them die. Further up the hill Lieutenant Higginson finds some mounted Basutos who have seen him coming and waited for him. Holding on to a horse's tail he finds running easier for a while, but he cannot maintain the pace for long and soon falls behind. Then he has another stroke of luck when he meets Trooper Barker of the Carbineers, who has seen him struggling from the top of the ridge and bravely ridden back to help. Higginson tells Barker that he has lost his horse and been injured crossing the river, so the trooper dismounts and helps him onto his own horse. Higginson immediately rides off at speed, leaving his rescuer to follow on foot.*

Back on the plain to the east of Isandlwana, the cavalrymen that Hamilton Browne has seen behind him still do not move. In fact they are the Mounted Infantry under Lieutenant-Colonel Russell, who have completed the reconnaissance to the north-east, which Lord Chelmsford ordered earlier, without encountering any significant enemy forces. They are now waiting for fresh orders. After a few minutes they move off, but eastward, in the direction of Mangeni rather than westward towards Browne.[16]

2:25 p.m. By this time the eclipse is over, and the sun is shining brightly again. There is no longer any co-ordinated resistance at Isandlwana, but it takes a long time to destroy an entire battalion of determined troops, and the last of the defenders are only now being hunted down and killed. Muziwento kaZibana[17] will be told later how the British soldiers face their ends in different ways; some fight to the death even though already badly wounded, wielding their bayonets to protect their comrades. Some try to run away or hide in the tents. Others 'cover their faces with their hands, not wishing to see death'. A few, who speak some isiZulu, plead for their lives, asking 'What wrong have we done, Cetshwayo?' Nzuzi Mandla of the uVe[18] replies to one, 'How can we give you mercy when you have come to us and want to take away our country and eat us up?' Elsewhere, Zofikasho Zungu of the iNgobamakhosi[19] sees a line of soldiers standing shoulder to shoulder among the tents with bayonets in their hands, having first fired off all their ammunition and then wielded their rifles like clubs until they are

---

* The identity of the men who killed Melvill and Coghill has never been definitely established. Apparently, there were a few of the pursuers from Isandlwana still on the Natal side of the river, like those whom Smith-Dorrien saw, but the likelihood is that the killers were local villagers who had previously been regarded as friendly to the British. No doubt the evidence that an overwhelming Zulu victory had taken place on the far bank was enough to convince many to change sides.

The upper slopes of Isandlwana, from the south-east. It was probably around 2:45 that Captain Reginald Younghusband led the survivors of C Company down the hill in their last suicidal charge from the shoulder on the right.

broken. All meet the same fate: the Zulus take no prisoners. Captain Younghusband has managed to get the survivors of his C Company onto the slopes of Isandlwana Hill, where they take cover behind the rocks and shoot down any Zulu who tries to climb up to them. Nevertheless, fire from below is gradually reducing their numbers. Mehlokazulu and his comrades have been fighting the soldiers on the nek for what seems to him like 'a long time', but now the British are beginning to run out of ammunition. One soldier has taken up a position between two aloe trees, whose spines make it difficult to approach him, and behind which he dodges whenever a spear is thrown at him. He seems to have plenty of rounds left, and soon there is a pile of dead Zulus in front of him.[20] Mlamula Matebula of the iNgobamakhosi regiment is behind several other warriors who are trying to rush him, but a couple of them are shot and the others in the front rank hesitate briefly. Mlamula pushes past them; the soldier does not see him until too late, and he manages to get within stabbing range and deliver the fatal blow.

Major Gossett overtakes Harness and his artillery with an order from the general. He is to obey his original instructions and continue at once to Mangeni. But just as he prepares to do so Lieutenant-Colonel Russell arrives on the road with his Mounted Infantry. Thanks to Browne's messenger Russell is aware of what the NNC have seen at Isandlwana, and is horrified by the indecision he finds. He rides ahead with Gossett to find Lord Chelmsford and explain the seriousness of the situation to him in person.[21]

2:35 p.m. Chelmsford is finally persuaded by Russell that Pulleine is in trouble, and he sets off back towards Isandlwana to investigate, accompanied by his staff and an escort of volunteers and mounted policemen.[22]

2:45 p.m. Younghusband's men have finally expended the last of their cartridges. Their officer draws his sword, and swinging it around his head he leads a charge down the hill and into the encircling Zulus.[23] Perhaps he is trying to cut his way through to join the remnants of the men on the nek; perhaps he just decides to die heroically. A warrior of the uNokhenkhe sees his sword blade flashing in the sunlight and wonders if it is made of fire. But his comrades seize their chance to get above the British, and by the time the charge is halted by superior numbers their retreat has been cut off. 'They killed themselves by running down' concludes the anonymous warrior as they close in around them.[24] Younghusband himself, and his second-in-command George Hodson, get as far as the flatter ground at the bottom of the hill before they are overwhelmed and killed. Only one of his company escapes the massacre and manages to take cover in a cave in the hillside, the entrance to which is protected by large boulders. There he waits in

Looking towards the Biggarsberg Mountains from the modern road which runs between Rorke's Drift and Fugitives' Drift. Helpmekaar is about ten miles away beyond the skyline to the right. This is the country which the exhausted men who had escaped from Isandlwana via Sothondose's Drift had to negotiate – some of them on foot – in the hours following the battle.

silence. A few men from other units have managed to get to the top of Isandlwana Hill itself, but some of the uKhandempemvu follow them up, stab them and throw their bodies down. Muti Ntshangase, an officer of the uNokhenkhe, approaches one man, presumably a colonial, who speaks to him in isiZulu: 'Do not kill me in the sun, kill me in the shadows,' he says.[25] Muti ignores this strange request and stabs him, but the incident puzzles those Zulus who witness it. One of them, Manwanana Mchunu, will later recall that Muti 'went mad', was taken back to the king, and cured only with difficulty by some Shangaan doctors brought in specially for the job. Who the man who seemingly cursed him was will never be known.

3:00 p.m. After losing his horse to Lieutenant Higginson, Trooper Barker has run about three miles in the afternoon heat when he sees Lieutenant Charlie Raw and two of his comrades riding back towards him leading his horse. Higginson had caught up with them, and when they recognised Barker's mount and enquired about him he had confessed what he had done, explaining that he himself was too badly hurt to walk, but he knew Barker was fresh enough to run, and in any case was intending to send the horse back for him. Lieutenant Raw had immediately ordered one of his African troopers – whose reaction is not recorded – to dismount, put Higginson on that horse and brought Barker's animal back to him.[26]

At Helpmekaar Captain Rainforth has been waiting for his relief, Major Russell Upcher's D Company, which has only just arrived, and has still not finished his preparations for the march to Rorke's Drift when he sees the first fugitives arrive with the news of the disaster at Isandlwana.[27] Upcher and Rainforth realise what this might portend for the garrison at Rorke's Drift, and decide to set out immediately with both companies. Helpmekaar will have to fend for itself.

Otto Witt and George Smith, still lingering on Shiyane Hill, have spent the last hour watching what are obviously bodies of African troops moving in the direction of Rorke's Drift.[28] From the top of Shiyane they are still several miles distant and their identity is not certain, but the two men can see that there are three 'companies', each between 1,000 and 1,500 strong. Smith notes that as they descend towards the Mzinyathi they are firing into the bushes and caves on either side of the path, presumably to drive out any enemies who are hiding there or waiting in ambush. They rest for a while and take snuff, then cross the river by forming long lines with linked arms to support each other against the current, before re-forming on the

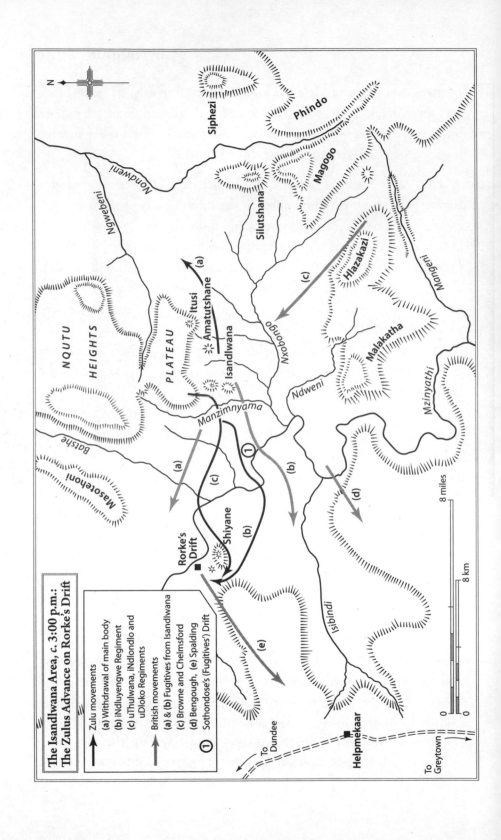

The Isandlwana Area, c. 3:00 p.m.:
The Zulus Advance on Rorke's Drift

Zulu movements
(a) Withdrawal of main body
(b) iNdluyengwe Regiment
(c) uThulwana, iNdlondlo and uDloko Regiments

British movements
(a) & (b) Fugitives from Isandlwana
(c) Browne and Chelmsford
(d) Bengough, (e) Spalding
① Sothondose's (Fugitives') Drift

NQUTU HEIGHTS

PLATEAU

Ngwebeni

Nondweni

Siphezi

Phindo

Magogo

Silutshana

Hlazakazi

Nxobongo

Amatutshane

Itusi

Isandlwana

Malakatha

Ndweni

Mzinyathi

Manzimnyama

Mangeni

Batshe

Masotehoni

Shiyane

Rorke's Drift

Isibindi

8 miles

8 km

To Dundee

Helpmekaar

To Greytown

N

Looking upstream along the Mzinyathi valley from the Fugitives' Drift road towards Rorke's Drift. On this stretch of the river the three Zulu regiments under the command of Prince Dabulamanzi crossed from right to left just before 3 p.m. They did so in the traditional manner, by linking arms to form a wedge formation and supporting each other as they battled against the current.

Natal side. Only now, as they come closer, can Witt and Smith see that, like the rank and file, the mounted officers who are leading them are black. As all the NNC officers are white men, these are evidently Zulus. The iNdluyengwe warriors are now hidden from sight, having crossed the Mzinyathi further downstream, so these must be Prince Dabulamanzi's three senior regiments approaching the river from the east. The two clergymen hastily follow Reynolds back towards

Rorke's Drift, scrambling over the boulders and between the spiny aloe bushes.*

3:10 p.m. Back at Rorke's Drift Lieutenant Chard is already aware of the danger, because as he rests in his tent overlooking the river he sees two men galloping towards him from the direction of Isandlwana. He goes out to meet them, and as soon as they have crossed the river one of them, Lieutenant Gert Adendorff of the NNC, takes him aside in a state of obvious agitation. Chard has taken off his tunic and is in his shirt sleeves, so Adendorff is not at first sure if he is talking to an officer, but when Chard identifies himself he blurts out the terrible news. The Zulus have captured the camp at Isandlwana, he tells him, and massacred the garrison. He adds that he is afraid that Lord Chelmsford and the rest of the army have suffered the same fate. Chard is at first sceptical and hints that Adendorff might have left the battlefield before he could see the outcome of the fighting, but his companion, a Carbineer, confirms the story. While they are still talking a messenger arrives from Bromhead at the post, asking Chard to come at once. Chard can now see that the fifty NNC men who were supposed to help defend the ponts have disappeared, having presumably already heard the news, so he posts the British NCO and his six men behind some rocks from where they can cover the river crossing, and runs to join Bromhead.[29]

3:20 p.m. Lieutenant Bromhead is holding an urgent conference with Surgeon Reynolds, Acting Assistant Commissary James Dalton and the other officers. He shows Chard Captain Gardner's note, which has just been brought in. There is a brief debate about the best way to respond to the threat. Bromhead has already ordered the wagons to be loaded in case it is necessary to abandon the post, but Dalton argues

---

* Witt's account is exceptionally confused but seems to suggest that he escaped from Shiyane on horseback, hotly pursued by Zulus. Anyone who has visited that rocky summit will find it difficult to believe that he got a horse up there at all, still less rode it away at a gallop.

Shiyane Hill seen from the direction of the Zulu advance from the south. The Rorke's Drift post is on the far side of the hill, and the Zulus approached it via the lower slopes to the left.

strongly against evacuation.[30] The Assistant Commissary is a retired former regular in his mid-forties, who emigrated to South Africa and has volunteered to serve in the commissariat department responsible for supplies. Therefore, although technically a civilian and subordinate to Walter Dunne, he is an experienced soldier and commands the respect of the regular officers. If they have to move at the pace of the wagons, he argues, they will soon be overtaken in the open, where there will be no chance of a successful defence. And leaving the wagons will mean abandoning the sick patients in the hospital, which is unthinkable as they know that the Zulus do not take prisoners. So the unanimous decision is made to stay and fight, and Chard begins to give the necessary orders. He is aware that the Witts' house, which is being used as the hospital, is a confusing warren of small rooms, some of which are accessible only from the outside. He orders his men to make loopholes in the external walls to improve the defenders' fields of fire, and to knock through the internal walls so that they can move freely inside the building to support each other and evacuate the patients if necessary. Unfortunately, the men are short of tools, time is pressing, and no officer can be spared to oversee the work. Although Chard does not realise this at the time, the second part of the job is not done.*

3:30 p.m. Luckily for the defenders of the mission station the place is full of stores which will make excellent improvised barricades. There are bags of mealie (or maize) meal, each weighing 200 pounds; biscuit boxes, about half that weight, but solidly constructed of wood; boxes of tinned meat, which are smaller than the biscuit boxes but at least as heavy; and even barrels of lime juice (intended to prevent scurvy) and rum. These are used to build barricades linking together the corners of the hospital and the storehouse, and running in front of the hospital as far as the north-western corner. Most of the work is done by Captain Stevenson's NNC, who with the addition of various additional men not formally allocated to organised units are now three or four hundred strong, but the British regulars willingly help to haul the heavy mealie sacks into position. Colour Sergeant Frank Bourne is only twenty-four years old and slightly built. Because of this, as he has discovered to his chagrin, the men refer to him behind his back as 'the kid'.[31] But he sets out with the authority conferred by his rank to post sentries in the hospital and at strategic points outside the perimeter. Sergeant Windridge undertakes the equally important duty of keeping

---

* Maps 7 and 8 show the approximate arrangement of the rooms inside the hospital, but the exact locations of any connecting doors, and the details of who was posted where, are not always clear. Numerous reconstructions of the subsequent events inside the building have been published, but the accounts of eyewitnesses are often inconsistent, and much must remain speculation.

an eye on the rum barrels which are still inside the storehouse while also loopholing the walls to provide a field of fire. A large water barrel is also filled and brought inside the yard enclosed by the defences. The supply wagons are built into the barricade on the southern side, facing Shiyane Hill. On the opposite side the obstacles run along the top of a natural rock wall, roughly the height of a man, which will add to the difficulty of climbing them. With the buildings themselves, and a stone cattle enclosure, or kraal, at the eastern end of the position, they will enclose the post on all sides.[32] The defences are perhaps partially bullet proof, but their greatest value will be in slowing down the advance of the enemy and preventing them from using their superior numbers to outflank the defenders.

Surgeon Reynolds is uncomfortably aware that the sick and wounded men in the hospital are at the most vulnerable end of the position and briefly considers moving them, but the other building is full of stores of various kinds which there is no time to move. Besides, he reassures himself, it is unlikely that either of these strongpoints will be lost unless the whole post falls.[33]

While the work of constructing these defences is going on, a growing stream of fugitives from Isandlwana passes the post, spreading more or less dramatised accounts of the disaster among the men before their officers can stop them. Surgeon Reynolds is assured by one of them that 'No power on earth can stand against the enormous numbers of Zulus' who are coming their way. A man named Doig of the Natal Mounted Police, on being asked by Trooper Harry Lugg for news, simply rides away with the prediction 'You will all be murdered.'[34] Another escapee remarks to Frank Bourne, 'Not a fighting chance for you, young fellow.' Chard is increasingly irritated by these prophets of doom, especially when the men stop work and gather round them to hear their unsettling tales. He does not bother to interrogate them himself or even to find out who they are, believing that in their state of demoralisation they are neither reliable sources of intelligence nor useful recruits to the garrison. He will later report that 'It is scarcely necessary for me to say that there were no officers of Her Majesty's Army among them.' [35]

Private Frederick Hitch is outside the post making tea for the garrison, and with remarkable coolness he decides to finish the job before the Zulus arrive. Meanwhile a man named Daniels, a civilian who is employed at Rorke's Drift as a ferryman, comes to Chard with a bold plan. He and Sergeant Milne, a Mounted Infantryman who has been working on the ponts, propose to moor them in the river upstream of the drift and defend them from there, where the Zulus will not be able to reach them. However, Chard has to refuse their brave offer, as he does not have enough men to hold the drift but intends to withdraw everyone within the post itself, from where they will not be able to see the ponts or support them with covering fire.

Commandant Rupert Lonsdale of the NNC is approaching Isandlwana from the east. He has been suffering from concussion after a fall from his horse, and has been given permission by Lord Chelmsford to return to the camp to rest.[36] In a semi-conscious state he rides to within a few hundred yards of his destination before he realises that it is full of Zulus; at the same time they become aware of him, and a group of them run towards him shouting and firing their muskets. Lonsdale is awake enough to turn his tired horse around and manages to persuade it to break into a canter, but it is several minutes before he leaves his pursuers behind. He sets off back towards Mangeni to warn the general.*

3:45 p.m. Otto Witt and Chaplain Smith have made their way back to Rorke's Drift to find preparations for a fight well under way. Witt is horrified at the damage being done to his house and furniture,

---

* Lonsdale's own account is rather more exciting, claiming that he rode right into the camp before being detected and only then came to his senses, finding himself surrounded by dead bodies belonging to both sides, torn tents and smashed ammunition boxes. He saw a Zulu rushing towards him with a bloodstained spear in his hand, and only managed to get away in the nick of time. It seems unlikely that he could have got so far without noticing the bodies of the Zulus who had fallen in the fight at the Nyogane donga, or that he could possibly have escaped if he had in fact been so close to the enemy. Norris Newman, who heard Lonsdale's oral report, got the impression that he had still been a few hundred yards from the camp when he saw that it was full of Zulus and turned back.

but Harry Lugg and his friends, with more urgent matters on their minds, merely find his agitation amusing. As a civilian Witt has no responsibilities at the post now that it is under military occupation, and he is concerned for the safety of his family whom he has left thirty miles away at Msinga, so he decides to leave while he still can. Smith at first considers leaving with him, but soon discovers that his horse (and coincidentally his groom) have disappeared, so he makes up his mind to stay and contribute to the defence as best he can.[37]

Chapter 6

The Siege of Rorke's Drift

'The deadly work now commenced.' *(Frederick Hitch)*

———◆———

4:00 p.m. Chard is relieved to see some more welcome arrivals from the direction of Isandlwana, as Lieutenant Henderson and about a hundred African troopers splash across the river at the drift and make their way up to the post. They are the Tlokoa from Durnford's force, and although understandably nervous they have kept their weapons and the appearance of military order. Chard asks Henderson to take them out to observe the Zulu advance and if possible to slow it down, using the volley and retire tactics that Colonel Durnford had employed a few hours earlier. They ride around the southern flank of Shiyane and disappear from sight.[1]

The victorious Zulus are beginning to drift away from the Isandlwana battlefield and back to the Nqutu Plateau. They load several hundred of their wounded into the captured wagons and begin to drag them up the slope; even if the Zulus were familiar with the techniques of inspanning and driving them, the oxen have all been killed or driven off. Hamilton Browne notes their laborious progress from a distance.[2] The lone anonymous survivor of Younghusband's company is still in his cave up on Isandlwana Hill, the last British soldier alive on the battlefield. He still has a supply of ammunition, perhaps taken from his dead comrades, and from inside his claustrophobic hideout he can see any Zulu who approaches over the boulders at the entrance silhouetted against the skyline.[3] He has already shot several of them, but from outside they cannot see him in the darkness and any return fire is wildly inaccurate.

At around this time the first messengers reach Cetshwayo's head-quarters at oNdini on horseback after a frantic four-hour ride, with news that the fighting has begun at Isandlwana. The king is worried, because no battle has been planned for today, but he begins the rituals which are necessary to ensure victory.[4] He goes to the hut where the grass rope coil, the '*inkatha yesizwe*', is kept. This incorporates the power of all his royal predecessors, and is the most powerful and sacred item that his people possess. His father's widows assure him that while he is seated on the *inkatha* he will be able to transmit this power to his warriors far away, but that if he abandons his post even for a moment it will be impossible for them to secure the victory. With growing anxiety, unable to issue orders, and aware that in fact the fighting must already be over one way or another, he waits for further news.

An increasingly anxious George Hamilton Browne finally sees a group of horsemen coming towards him from the east. But instead of the expected army it is a small group comprising Lord Chelmsford and a few of his staff who have ridden on ahead of their escort. Even now the general appears to blame Browne, rather than the Zulus, for the disruption to his plans.[5] 'What are you doing here Commandant Browne?' he demands. 'You ought to have been in the camp hours ago.' When Browne informs him that the camp has been taken by the enemy, the general snaps 'How dare you tell me such a falsehood? Get your men into line at once and advance.' Browne has no choice but to obey, so he deploys his 700 half-armed NNC and starts to lead them to their doom against the entire Zulu army. Chelmsford and the staff ride close behind.

4:15 p.m. There is a brief outbreak of firing behind Shiyane Hill, and moments later Henderson's troopers come back at a gallop. The first clash with the enemy has proved too much for their already battered morale, their ammunition is running low, and after the death of their respected commander, Anthony Durnford, they can see no reason to continue the fight. The Tlokoa keep going past the post in the direction of Helpmekaar, while Lieutenant Henderson – perhaps more for the sake of appearances than anything – stops and fires a few shots at an enemy whom the garrison still cannot see, before following his men's

The entrance to one of the caves in the ledge on Shiyane Hill. It was in one of these dark, cramped holes that Chard's mule driver managed to escape detection throughout the battle.

example. Even more seriously, the panic also infects Stevenson's assorted NNC levies, most of whom have never considered themselves to be combat troops. They suddenly drop whatever they are carrying, jump over the barricades and run after the Tlokoa in a body.[6] Meanwhile, Frederick Hitch gets safely inside the perimeter with his rifle and four kettles of much needed tea. Stevenson and their white NCOs then follow their men in flight, much to the disgust of the remaining defenders. Hitch and some others are so enraged that they fire their rifles at them as they run. One of the NCOs, Corporal Anderson, is seen to fall forward, shot through the head. No one is sure who fired the shot, but by an unspoken agreement the defenders decide to say no more about the matter.[7]

Within minutes the garrison of 450 men has been reduced by two-thirds. Bourne's pickets run back inside the perimeter at the prospect of the imminent arrival of the enemy. Lieutenant Chard's wagon driver has brought his vehicle up from the drift and unharnessed the mules, but decides not to wait and share the fate of the garrison. He runs up onto the rocky terrace on Shiyane which overlooks the post and hurriedly ducks into one of the shallow caves in the slope behind.[8]

4:20 p.m. Lieutenant Bromhead has ordered Hitch to climb onto the roof of the storehouse and give warning of the enemy's approach. From his elevated position he is the first to see the advance skirmishers of the iNdluyengwe regiment forming into their battle formation just beyond the flank of Shiyane Hill.[9] As they come into sight they are about 800 yards distant. They are advancing at a trot, in silence; each man in the leading wave appears to carry a gun in his hand and has slung his spears over his back. They extend into open order and continue their advance without checking their pace. Hitch quickly shouts a warning to Bromhead, standing on the ground below, and the officer asks him how many Zulus there are. Hitch can only see the lead regiment at this point. The iNdluyengwe are perhaps 700 strong, but their numbers are difficult to estimate and more are coming around the hill every minute. Surgeon Reynolds, spotting them from ground level moments later, thinks of them as 'an innumerable swarm'. There are between four and six thousand, an understandably excited Hitch tells his officer. This cannot be encouraging news for Bromhead, but an officer's duty is to keep up an imperturbable front even in the direst straits. 'Is that all?' he shouts back, 'We can manage that lot very well!'*

Browne and Chelmsford are now close enough to the remains of the camp at Isandlwana that the general can no longer avoid the

---

* Hitch's account (for which see Boucher [1973]) is not clearly punctuated and Bromhead's remark, as quoted there in its entirety, can be interpreted in two different ways: "'We can manage that lot very well for a few seconds." There were other opinions...' Or "'We can manage that lot very well." For a few seconds there were other opinions.' Most authorities have gone with the first version, but there is a gallows humour about it that seems much less appropriate than the second for raising morale.

The church at Rorke's Drift, the storehouse at the time of the battle, seen from the south-west. This would have been the view obtained by the advance skirmishers of the iNdluyengwe regiment as they came round the shoulder of Shiyane at about 4:30. The British barricade extended to the left of the building, in the direction of the hospital.

---

truth. In what Browne will remember as a 'kindly manner', Chelms-ford calls out and asks him 'On your honour, Commandant Browne, is the camp taken?'[10] Browne replies that it was taken at about 1:30, nearly three hours ago, and the smoke that they can now see is due to the Zulus burning the tents. Even so Chelmsford's instinct is to deny the possibility of disaster, and he remarks that it could be the quarter-master's fatigue party burning rubbish. Browne is by now struggling to remain calm and respectful. 'QM's fatigue do not burn tents, sir,' he replies, and hands his field glasses to the general. Chelmsford refuses them, but says 'Halt your men at once.' The relieved NNC take up a defensive position while the commander-in-chief despatches the much travelled Major Gossett with orders to bring back Colonel Glyn and the rest of the column from Mangeni.

As Browne's men settle down to wait once more, Commandant Lonsdale arrives from the direction of Isandlwana, worn out and on foot, leading an even more exhausted pony. He confirms to Browne that there are Zulus in the camp, and is immediately sent on to tell his story to the staff. Even then Chelmsford struggles to take in the extent of the disaster, and Lonsdale's impression is that Chelmsford thinks he is still suffering from concussion. 'I can't understand it,' the general is heard to mutter, 'I left a thousand men to guard the camp.'[11]

Major Bengough and his NNC battalion are still holding their position on the banks of the Mzinyathi. The artillery fire which they could hear to the north has long since ceased, and all is quiet. Then the major's interpreter interrupts his thoughts with a worrying report. He has encountered a local Zulu who has told him that the 'English *impi*' has been 'eaten up' at Isandlwana and its chief killed. A Zulu army, he adds, is even now on its way to destroy Bengough's force.[12] This last detail is incorrect, as by now the victorious Zulus have either retired in the opposite direction or crossed the river further north, on their way to Rorke's Drift. But Bengough dares not take any chances. He decides that their present position on the Zululand bank is not defensible, and that, as the river is easily fordable in several places, they would not be able to prevent a Zulu crossing from there. So he orders his column to cross back to the Natal side to take up a defensive position on the higher ground there.*

Six or seven miles to the west, still on the road to Helpmekaar, Major Spalding meets two companies of redcoats marching in the

---

* Historical 'what ifs' are always difficult to evaluate, but it is tempting to speculate what this enthusiastic NNC battalion, under its experienced commander, could have done to retrieve the situation at either Isandlwana or Rorke's Drift. Alternatively, if it had remained under Durnford's command it might have done good service reconnoitring on his northern flank. As it was it has been left stranded by a succession of orders and counter-orders, and has wasted the entire day in a position from where it could influence neither battle.

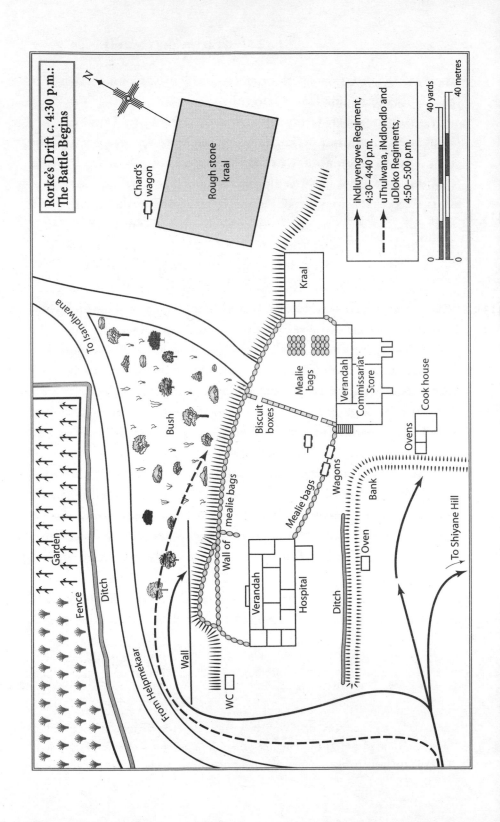

Rorke's Drift c. 4:30 p.m.: The Battle Begins

N

Chard's wagon

Rough stone kraal

To Isandlwana

From Helpmekaar

Garden

Fence

Ditch

Wall

WC

Bush

Wall of mealie bags

Biscuit boxes

Mealie bags

Verandah

Commissariat Store

Kraal

Mealie bags

Wagons

Mealie bags

Verandah

Hospital

Ditch

Oven

Bank

Ovens

Cook house

To Shiyane Hill

→ iNdluyengwe Regiment, 4:30–4:40 p.m.

- - → uThulwana, iNdlondlo and uDloko Regiments, 4:50–5:00 p.m.

0 ___ 40 yards

0 ___ 40 metres

opposite direction. They are the reinforcements he has been looking for – D and G Companies of the 1/24th, commanded by Upcher and Rainforth. But Spalding, who until now has had no inkling of the danger in which he has left his command, is horrified to learn the reason why they are on the road. He immediately turns around and marches back with them.[13]

4:30 p.m. As the iNdluyengwe come within range of Rorke's Drift the first shots are exchanged. Several of the Zulu skirmishers spot Private Hitch on the roof and fire at him, but the rounds either go over his head or bury themselves in the wall of the storehouse.[14]

4:35 p.m. Chard's wagon driver is horrified to see several Zulus enter his cave and lie down in the entrance, aiming their muskets at the British below. With their eyes unaccustomed to the darkness they fail to spot him, but he cowers terrified at the far end of the cave, scarcely daring to breathe. From his position on the roof Hitch can see that several groups of Zulus are moving to their right and occupying firing positions among the rocks on the hill; one of them, apparently an officer, seems to be counting the defenders. Hitch fires at him, but his shot falls short. The *induna* then shifts his position to the right and gives a signal with his arm. Hitch has no time to adjust his sights because he has to keep Lieutenant Bromhead informed of the increasingly ominous developments: as well as firing down into the post from Shiyane the enemy are also veering to their left and beginning to threaten the front wall. It looks as though in a very short time the defenders will be surrounded. Hitch will later describe the enemy deployment as 'in the shape of a bullock's horn', in other words the classic Zulu envelopment which has already proven so deadly at Isandlwana. From Reynolds's point of view the formation looks like 'a giant pair of nutcrackers' poised to crush the little post.[15] The defenders on the ground fire their first shots at the extreme range of 800 yards and cause few casualties. To Reynolds things are now looking 'nasty, really nasty'. He is concerned to see that the initial volley does not slow the Zulu advance at all; they just keep coming at a steady trot. Gunner Arthur Howard, defending the hospital, makes a pact with his comrades that they will fight on until only two of them are left, and these last two will shoot themselves to avoid capture.[16] Howard is the batman (or servant) of Lieutenant-Colonel Harness, who is with Lord Chelmsford; he has been left behind in the hospital suffering from dysentery, but is fit enough to take up a rifle and join in the defence. The range is closing at a little over a hundred yards a minute, and at 600 yards the crack shots among the defenders start to pick off their targets. Private Dunbar gives a spectacular demonstration of marksmanship, hitting eight men with successive shots, one of them a mounted *induna* who is seen to topple off his horse.[17] At 400 yards Gunner Howard and his friends join in the firing, and their spirits begin to lift as they see the Zulus fall. Harry Lugg is using a carbine with a broken stock, but is pleased to see that its accuracy is not affected; at 350 yards he takes aim at a Zulu and sees him fall. Another expert shot is Private Alfred Hook, who engages one of the iNdluyengwe hiding behind an anthill 300 yards away. Hook's first shot goes over his head as he raises it to look out, then the second hits the ground a few paces short. But now Hook has the range, and when the man's head appears again he fires his third shot, and the Zulu disappears, never to re-emerge.[18]

4:40 p.m. So far the warriors of the iNdluyengwe have been advancing in a cool and professional manner, 'just as British soldiers would do', thinks Private John Waters.[19] Taking advantage of the anthills and shrubs that the defenders have not had time to clear, and giving each other covering fire from these positions to supplement the hail of bullets coming from the commanding height of Shiyane, a group of them reach the shelter of the cookhouse just outside the perimeter. From there the Zulus fire a series of volleys at the back wall of the hospital, but the soldiers manning the hospital and the storehouse have them in a crossfire and they are unable to advance any further. Corporal Attwood of the Army Service Corps, firing downwards from an upper window of the storehouse, hits a Zulu on the crown of the head as he runs forward in a crouch, and sees the exiting bullet blow half his face away, making 'an awful mess' that he will recall even years later.[20] Hitch finds that the attackers are too close to his own comrades for him to be able to shoot effectively from his perch on the roof, so he descends and joins the line fighting down below, fixing his bayonet as he runs. One of those defending the storehouse is Lieutenant Adendorff, the fugitive from Isandlwana, who is now facing his second battle of the day. Despite the trauma from which he is already suffering he maintains a steady, accurate fire.*

With the defenders' Martini Henrys firing at 300 yards and less, the Zulu casualty list is growing, and eventually the entire iNdluyengwe regiment is forced to ground. By now, however, many of the Zulus have taken cover within fifty yards of the post, and have extended their line along the north wall so as to almost completely surround it. James Dalton has quickly reverted to his old role as a fighting soldier. He climbs onto one of the wagons which have been built into the perimeter on the side facing Shiyane and hurls insults at the enemy in the hope of provoking them to break cover. When they do not respond, having no ammunition to hand, he throws his helmet at them in a fighting rage. For the present, Dalton remains miraculously unscathed.[21]

4:50 p.m. Dabulamanzi's other three Zulu regiments are all composed of older men than the iNdluyengwe, and their advance across country has been slightly slower, but by now they are beginning to arrive on the scene, and their leading elements are following their predecessors round the shoulder of Shiyane Hill. They spread out to reinforce the men of the iNdluyengwe who are facing the north side of the post, in front of the hospital, and immediately launch a succession of ferocious

* The role of Lieutenant Adendorff has always been controversial, since most participants at Rorke's Drift appear not to have noticed his presence. He was later accused of having deserted from both battles, though no court martial ever took place. In an engagement like this one, where men were often fighting from cover in isolated positions, it would not be surprising if some were completely unaware of the actions of others. If he had ridden off on horseback before the Zulus closed in, however, someone would surely have seen him do so. Therefore I have preferred the testimony of Lieutenant Chard, who ought to have known who was under his command, and who made a point in his report to Queen Victoria of mentioning the 'good service' performed by Adendorff at this stage in the fight.

assaults against the wall of mealie bags on top of the rocky ledge. A series of desperate hand-to-hand fights ensues.[22]

Major Gossett is now approaching the improvised camp site at Mangeni where Glyn and the rest of the 2nd/24th are preparing to bivouac. Gossett reins in his horse so that his frantic pace will not cause alarm, but Glyn comes to meet him, already fearing the worst. Chelmsford's message informs him that the Zulus have got into the camp at Isandlwana and that he is to march there at once.[23]

5:00 p.m. The firefight intensifies between the Zulu snipers on Shiyane Hill and the British soldiers manning the south wall of the post. The snipers are now being reinforced by men from the three newly arrived regiments, and although the defenders facing them are largely protected by the barricade, the Zulus have a clear view of the backs of the soldiers manning the north wall on the far side of the post, who are facing away from them. However, the range is between 300 and 400 yards, which is much too great for aimed fire with the Zulus' obsolete muskets. All they can do is point their weapons in the general direction and trust to luck, hoping not to overshoot and hit their own men on the other side of the barricades. Meanwhile the British rifles are highly accurate at this range, and although the Zulus are taking cover in caves and behind rocks, the clouds of smoke from their muskets give away their positions. The soldiers on the south wall, among whom is the crack shot Private Dunbar, inflict heavy losses on them.

Chard's wagon driver, still trapped in his cave, sees one of the Zulus at the entrance knocked backward by the impact of a British bullet; he realises that he is in as much danger now from friendly fire as he is from the enemy, not to mention the scorpions that lurk in the dark recesses, but with enemy warriors blocking the only way out he has no option but to remain where he is.

A dozen or so Zulus have picked up Martini Henrys from the Isandlwana battlefield, probably from the bodies of Dyson's men who were lying on the spur above the camp when they passed by, along with a few cartridges each. They are not familiar with the sights or the

Taken from the ledge where the Zulu sharpshooters took up their firing positions on Shiyane, this picture may give an idea of the difficulties that they faced when shooting down into the post. The range to the hospital and storehouse – the two buildings just this side of the road in the centre – is between 200 and 300 yards. This was more than twice the effective range of a smoothbore musket, and although there are places along the north and south walls where the defenders would have been very exposed, elsewhere the lines of sight were at least partially blocked by the buildings. What is more, the British Martini Henry rifles, with their flatter trajectory, were highly effective at this distance, and even if the Zulus took cover in the caves or behind the rocks their position would inevitably be betrayed by the clouds of white smoke from their weapons.

———

ballistics of the weapon, and as is their usual habit they raise the sights to maximum range in the belief that this will increase the impact of the bullets. Consequently all their shots fly well over the post and they cause no casualties, except possibly a few to their own men, but Colour Sergeant Bourne hears the distinctive report of the rifles and concludes that large numbers of captured weapons are being used against the garrison.*

5:15 p.m. Despite the occasional casualty from the Zulu muskets, the defenders hold their positions along the north wall, and each enemy rush is met by a hedge of British bayonets. It is the bayonet, rather than the bullet, that is the decisive weapon in this phase of the fight. The reach of the rifle and fixed bayonet is much greater than that of the short Zulu stabbing spear, especially when wielded by a man standing on higher ground and with his lower body protected by the mealie bags. Private Hitch notes that the enemy seems to have 'a great dread of the bayonet'. This is not surprising as the Zulu military system depends ultimately on their superiority in close-quarters combat; they have always overcome African opponents who rely on throwing spears, and the only white troops against whom they have had any experience until now are the Boers, who are just as vulnerable at close range as they do not use the bayonet themselves. Now, for the first time, Dabulamanzi's regiments are facing regular soldiers who can not only outshoot them, but also outmatch them man for man in a hand-to-hand fight. Some warriors try to snatch the soldiers' rifles or bayonets and use them against them, but are shot at point-blank range in the process. One throws down his weapons and grabs Hitch's Martini Henry in both hands, but Hitch somehow manages to load the rifle and kill the man even as he wrestles with him. A handful of the more athletic Zulus leap right over the mealie bag parapet, but with their comrades unable to get over to support them they are all quickly killed. In between rushes, the attackers take cover in the bushes below the ledge and fire their

* Many writers have attempted to reconcile Bourne's categorical statement that the enemy employed captured Martini Henrys at Rorke's Drift with the equally definite casualty reports after the battle, which mention only wounds from smoothbore guns and spears. Alternatively, they have argued that Bourne was simply mistaken, but in view of his combat experience, and his later career as a musketry instructor, he ought to have known what a British rifle sounded like. The above seems the most likely explanation for the contradictions in the sources.

muskets at close range. This, rather than the sniping from Shiyane, is the cause of most of the British casualties at this stage of the fight.

Not every man among the defenders is an experienced combat veteran. Major Spalding's clerk, Sergeant George Mabin, has never killed anyone in his life before, but now he sees a big Zulu coming straight towards him with his spear ready for action. The warrior advances in a series of short rushes, taking cover at every opportunity, but when he dives behind a large boulder Mabin covers the rock with his rifle and waits. Suddenly the Zulu springs to his feet and prepares to close in for the kill, but the sergeant pulls the trigger and sees his opponent leap into the air and fall dead.[24]

George Smith, who is a clergyman of the 'Praise the Lord and pass the ammunition' school, is doing just that, handing out cartridges to the men and exhorting them not to swear but rather to keep shooting. Adendorff overhears an exchange between the chaplain and an unnamed 'hard case' among the soldiers, who is cursing loudly as he loads and fires. Smith urges him to mind his language, reminding him – as if it were necessary – that they might soon be meeting their Maker and have to answer for their sins.[25]

At Mangeni Colonel Glyn has little in the way of equipment to pack up, and his infantry companies are already on their way back to Isandlwana, followed by Harness and his long-suffering gun teams, retracing their steps yet again. The men cannot yet know of the fate of the comrades whom they left behind only this morning, let alone the crisis at Rorke's Drift, but they are aware that things have gone badly wrong, and they make good speed along the well-trodden trail.[26]

Six miles ahead of them at Isandlwana, the shadows are growing long and most of the Zulus have long since left the scene of their victory. But the lone survivor of C Company is still alive, and still shooting at anyone who wanders within range. A group of warriors decide that it is time to finish the business. They take up positions on the slope below and fire repeated volleys into the cave with Martini Henry rifles taken from the countless dead redcoats. Although their target is invisible, the high velocity rounds will ricochet off the rock

The hospital from the north, with Shiyane in the background. The building was protected by a row of mealie bags, whose location is marked by the row of stones in front of it. The small semi-circular projection that was added to strengthen this weak spot in the defences is also indicated by stones at centre left.

walls until eventually they hit something. At last no more shots are returned from inside.[27]

5:30 p.m. The section of barricade just in front of the hospital at Rorke's Drift has been hastily constructed and the rocky ledge here is lower, so several groups of Zulus manage to jump over the mealie bags and get inside the compound. They are all despatched by a small reserve of riflemen, among whom Bromhead, Bourne and Dalton are conspicuous. It occurs to Colour Sergeant Bourne to wonder why the Zulus do not cut open the mealie bags from below with their assegais and so collapse the barricade. He concludes that their proverbial cunning has deserted them on this occasion. But from the perspective of the Zulus below it is not the mealie bags that are the problem; even without them the man-high ledge lined at the top with bayonets is quite enough of an obstacle. And if the contents of the bags were to be spilled they would simply make the ground underfoot even more treacherous.

Privates Hook and Cole are stationed in a small room at the south-western corner of the hospital, otherwise occupied only by one of the patients, an isiGqoza from the NNC with a badly broken leg. Cole is frustrated by the lack of targets visible from the loopholes, and he can hear the noise of the main attack going in against the north wall behind him. He suddenly announces that he is going outside. This room at least has an internal door giving access to the main internal space – formerly the Witts' living room – and thus to the veranda on the north side, so he ducks out that way, leaving Hook with only the helpless isiGqoza for company.[28]

5:40 p.m. Cole manages to make his escape to the veranda and join the defenders there, but moments later they are forced to evacuate this section of the perimeter and fall back towards the main yard. Fortunately Chard has had the forethought to construct a short line of mealie bags linking the north-west corner of the hospital to the main defensive line, and this becomes the new front line. Less fortunately, this allows the Zulus to get right up to the front of the hospital.[29] The men inside the building are firing from their isolated rooms through loopholes, but these provide only a limited field of fire, and they are unable to drive the enemy away from the building. At some point during this struggle, Cole is killed by a musket shot to the head.[30] Alongside Chard, James Dalton is conspicuous in the defence of the north wall outside the hospital, striding along the line regardless of his own safety and employing his rifle wherever the threat is greatest. He sees two Zulus charging towards him, and takes aim at one while indicating the other to his companions with the instruction 'Pot that fellow!'[31] Someone does, but suddenly Dalton turns round and hands his rifle to Chard, remarking quite calmly that he has been shot.

Surgeon Reynolds, running to his side, finds that a musket ball has gone completely through his shoulder. He helps him away from the perimeter.

6:00 p.m. As the latest assault on the mealie bag rampart is repulsed, Chard realises that it is only a matter of time before the Zulus break in. They will have to retire to the second line of defence, a line of biscuit boxes which he has had built across the yard, linking the north wall with the corner of the storehouse. It is not an easy decision, as it means abandoning the hospital. The handful of able-bodied defenders still in the building might be able to make their escape, but there is no way to warn them. As for the sick and wounded, their prospects seem even more hopeless. But Chard's primary duty is to the defenders under his immediate command, and the only way to save them is to contract the perimeter.[32] He gives the order, and the men lining the barricade on the north side of the yard start to fall back.

The messengers arriving at oNdini are beginning to bring good news; when they left, some four and a half hours earlier, the battle was clearly going in favour of the Zulus. Cetshwayo, in mounting impatience, cannot resist going out to speak to them, in spite of the warnings from the ladies of his household.[33]

6:30 p.m. The Zulus are throwing spears wrapped with burning grass onto the thatched roof of the hospital in an attempt to set it alight and force the defenders to evacuate the building. The attempt is not successful at first as the thatch is damp from recent rains, but after a few minutes it begins to smoulder. This is an unexpected stroke of luck for the defenders. They still do not know that Chard's withdrawal to the biscuit box line has left them isolated, but as the smoke seeps from the roof they understand that they need to get out. Some of them are in a position to break out over the veranda. Gunner Howard spots an opportunity while the Zulus' attention is elsewhere, jumps over the mealie bags and the stone wall beyond, and takes cover in the shelter of a group of dead horses which have been caught in the crossfire outside the perimeter.[34]

Chard's last line of defence, the biscuit-box barricade, ran from the north wall to the corner of the storehouse as indicated by this double row of stones. The hospital is out of view to the right. It is clear from the section of Shiyane Hill visible just to the right of the storehouse that the men lining this barricade were still vulnerable to enfilade fire from the Zulus on the ledge, although less so than when they had been manning the north wall with their backs to the hill.

6:35 p.m. Private Roy and another soldier follow Howard out onto the hospital veranda, Roy fixing his bayonet as he runs because his rifle has jammed. They veer to the right and make a run for the biscuit-box line, but they are spotted. A group of Zulus rushes after them – Roy has no time to look back and count them, though he later estimates that there were as many as thirty – but their comrades behind the barricade give them covering fire and they succeed in getting to safety. One of the patients, Private Beckett, runs out next, but by sheer bad luck he

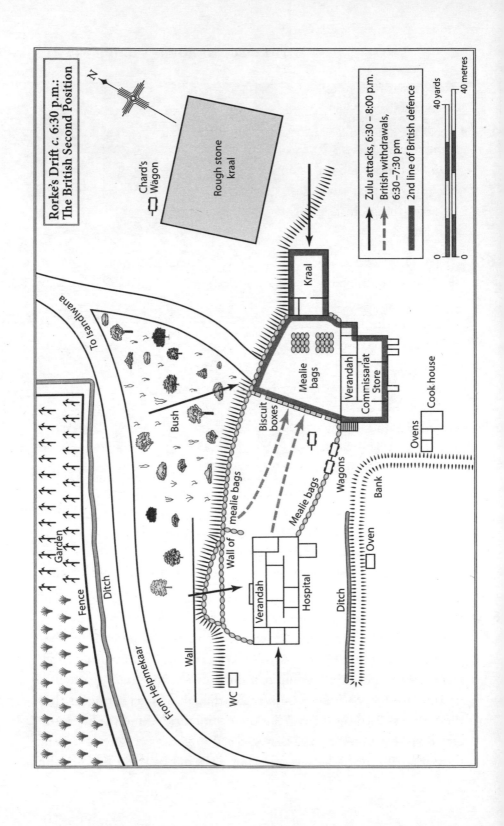

Rorke's Drift c. 6:30 p.m.:
The British Second Position

N

Chard's Wagon

Rough stone kraal

Zulu attacks, 6:30 – 8:00 p.m.
British withdrawals, 6:30–7:30 pm
2nd line of British defence

0   40 yards

0   40 metres

To Isandlwana

Garden

Fence

Ditch

From Helpmekaar

Bush

Wall

WC

Wall of mealie bags

Verandah

Hospital

Ditch

Oven

Bank

Mealie bags

Wagons

Biscuit boxes

Mealie bags

Kraal

Verandah

Commissariat Store

Ovens

Cook house

collides with a Zulu on the veranda. In a reflex action the surprised warrior stabs him in the stomach with his spear, but Beckett stays on his feet long enough to jump the barricade and follow Howard into the bushes below.[35] John Waters, who was wounded earlier fighting on the perimeter, has been defending the front of the hospital with Beckett, but realising that the line of retreat via the veranda is now blocked, he takes refuge in a small room at the north-western corner of the building.[36]

6:45 p.m. East of Isandlwana Glyn's column catches up with Chelmsford, who is still observing the camp from a safe distance, and the general starts to deploy the whole force into line of battle. He places his guns in the centre, with the regular infantry on either side of them, then Browne's and Cooper's NNC battalions on the flanks, and the mounted troops further out to either side. Then he addresses the men, telling them that the Zulus have captured the camp and all the stores, and that they must retake them with the bayonet before pressing on to Rorke's Drift. He says nothing about the men who were left to defend the camp, and it is likely that at this point everyone still prefers to believe that they have fallen back on the river crossing and will be waiting there to meet them. The men raise a cheer and begin their advance.[37]

Captain Edward Essex, arriving at Helpmekaar from the catastrophe at Isandlwana, finds Upcher's company, which was supposed to be garrisoning it, gone, and the place completely unprepared for defence. He knows only too well the consequences of such unpreparedness in the face of the Zulus, and at once orders a *laager* of ox wagons to be made.[38]

John Waters has managed to stay undetected while shooting several Zulus who have broken into the hospital and are now on their way out again to escape the fire, but as the smoke becomes thicker he realises that it is time for him to leave. The room he is in has evidently been used by the Reverend Witt as a cloakroom, because his black clerical cloak is still in there. Waters has the presence of mind to wrap himself in this before following in the footsteps of Howard and Beckett and throwing himself down in the long grass outside the post, where he is almost invisible in the gathering darkness.*

6:50 p.m. Meanwhile three other privates, William Horrigan and Joseph and John Williams, have been firing through loopholes from a room at the western end of the hospital, which also holds four non-combatant patients.[39] There is no internal door to this room, so John Williams (who has enlisted under a false name – his real name is Fielding) is belatedly following Chard's instructions and knocking a hole in the wall with a pick, through which he hopes to evacuate the patients. Luckily the internal walls are flimsily built from mud brick, and the work progresses quickly. John's namesake Joseph Williams is a deadly shot who has already killed fourteen Zulus (the bodies will be found outside his position the next morning), but now he is out of ammunition and he is forced to try and block the doorway with his bayonet. Suddenly a powerful arm grabs him, and Horrigan and John Williams are horrified to see him dragged outside, where he is quickly

---

* Lieutenant Chard, in his report to the Queen, relates a story that Waters somehow 'made his way to the cookhouse', which he found was occupied by Zulus who were firing in the direction of the post. Nevertheless, he sneaked in to the fireplace undetected, stood up in the chimney and covered his hands and face with soot. There he is said to have stood all night, only emerging in the morning, when he was nearly mistaken for a Zulu by the defenders and shot. Chard implies that he heard this story from Waters himself, but it is difficult to know what to make of it. The cookhouse was on the opposite side of the post from the room in the hospital where he had been hiding, and no reason is given for him undertaking the journey when the relative safety of the defended biscuit box barricade was so much closer. It would in any case have been almost impossible for him to have walked or crawled so far round the outside of the perimeter without running into a Zulu on the way. We are further expected to believe that Waters got inside the cookhouse – presumably by the only door – spotted its occupants, and wandered about inside this very small building without them noticing him. This is in addition to the question raised by Mike Snook, of whether such an edifice would even have had a proper chimney. The whole account seems improbable, and here I follow Colonel Snook in rejecting it entirely.

surrounded and stabbed to death. Horrigan somehow breaks out into the open, where Private Waters, looking back towards the post, sees him also speared. John Williams manages to drag two of the patients through the hole he has made into the living room, but is forced to leave the other two, Privates Adams and Hayden, behind to be slaughtered as the Zulus burst into the room. Hayden's body will later be found with sixteen stab wounds.

7:00 p.m. It is beginning to get dark, but as Chelmsford's men reach the Nyogane donga large numbers of Zulus can still be seen evacuating the camp area and retiring over the escarpment to the right. Here the British troops begin to realise the extent of the disaster as they encounter the first corpses, initially widely scattered, but lying in dense masses as they get closer to the nek. No targets are visible in the gloom, but Chelmsford orders Harness to unlimber the guns and fire into the camp. Hamilton Browne is ordered to seize the top of Mahlabamkhosi Hill, but has great difficulty in persuading his terrified men to advance. Only a company of the 24th coming up behind them with fixed bayonets induces them to climb the hill, but when they reach the top they find it unoccupied.[40]

7:10 p.m. Chard realises that even his smaller perimeter is at risk of being overrun, so he gives the order to construct a 'redoubt' out of two piles of mealie bags which have been left in the yard next to the storehouse. This can be used to provide some shelter for the wounded, and if the worst comes to the worst will form a rallying point for a final stand. Commissary Walter Dunne and a handful of men begin the task of moving the 200-pound mealie bags, Dunne standing on top of the piles and heaving the bags into the space between them. He is particularly vulnerable in this position, silhouetted against the burning hospital, especially since the Zulus are firing high, but somehow he is not hit. He notices that the small birds which have been nesting in the thatched roofs have been disturbed by the noise and the smoke, and are flying agitatedly around his head.[41]

7:20 p.m. Alfred Hook has been defending his position in the hospital alone since Cole left, but now, with the roof on fire and the Zulus threatening to batter down the external door, he is forced to retire through an internal door into the room behind him.[42] He slams the door shut and drags a wooden bed against it, briefly deterring the Zulus from trying to batter it open by firing a shot through the woodwork. He has had no time to help the injured isiGqoza, and is now forced to listen to a brief conversation in isiZulu as the attackers try to interrogate him, followed by the sounds of him being stabbed to death as he tries to escape. Hook's new position is one of a series of small rooms on the south side of the hospital, occupied by a number of patients including Private John Connolly, who has a dislocated knee. This room also connects with the larger living room to Hook's left, and from this direction comes John Williams, still in shock at the death of his comrade Joseph. However, Williams still has his pick, and with it he starts to make another hole in the east wall of the room while Hook tries to defend both doors.

As the attacking Zulus break open the door through which he has come, Hook finds himself fighting desperately against superior numbers. He survives only because the doorway is too narrow for more than one man to pass through it at a time. Some of the Zulus throw spears, but in the confined space there is no room to aim them properly and all but one miss their target; that one hits Hook on the helmet and inflicts a scalp wound, but at the moment he is too busy to even notice it. Another warrior grabs Hook's rifle and tries to snatch it off him, but Hook's grip on the stock is firmer and he manages to load the weapon and fire it with the muzzle touching the man's chest. Somehow he succeeds in shooting or bayoneting every man who comes through the door. He does not have time to count them, but there are five or six dead Zulus lying at his feet by the time he sees that Williams and most of the patients have broken through the far wall via a small hole at ground level and reached the room beyond. Hook is now literally wading in blood. The only patient remaining is Private Connolly,

The yard and the hospital, as seen from the site of the biscuit-box barricade. Surgeon Reynolds crossed this exposed space, illuminated by the flames of the burning roof and under fire by Zulus along the north wall to the right, to resupply the men in the building with ammunition. Shortly afterwards, at around 7:30, the sick and wounded from the hospital were evacuated through a small window in the wall facing the camera.

whose injured leg makes him difficult to move, but Hook scrambles through the hole in the wall and simply drags the man after him. In the process he dislocates Connolly's knee again, causing him agonising pain, but at least he has been spared the fates of the patients left behind in the other rooms.

Williams continues with his work, smashing another hole into the next and last room on that side of the building, while Hook stands over the previous hole with his bayonet. This position is easier to defend than an open door, but for a few moments, astonishingly, the Zulus keep trying to crawl through the little hole. Hook despatches every one. Then Hook and Williams are through into the larger room at the south-eastern corner of the building, bringing a procession of ten patients with them, out of the frying pan and into the fire. Here two able-bodied soldiers, William and Robert Jones, are out of ammunition and trying to prevent the Zulus outside from breaking in the external door, while another five disabled hospital patients watch in mounting terror. There is a window in the external wall on the eastern side, which gives access to the courtyard, and thirty yards away to the biscuit box barricade, but the window is high up in the wall and the sick and injured will struggle to reach it. At this point Surgeon Reynolds makes a heroic dash across the open yard from the biscuit box line to pass packets of rifle cartridges through the window to the defenders. Although the Zulus on the far side of the mealie bags to his right are firing at him he somehow gets back unscathed, one musket ball glancing off his helmet as he runs.[43]

7:30 p.m. As the hospital door bursts open the Zulus try to rush in, but William and Robert Jones cross their bayonets and stab every man who comes through. Robert receives three spear wounds in the process, but remains on his feet. While they keep the enemy at bay, Alfred Hook and John Williams help the patients up to the window and through it into the yard. One of the first out is a Natal Mounted Policeman named Hunter, who hesitates for a moment, perhaps stunned by the fall or dazed by the glare of the burning roof. A Zulu lying in wait behind the north wall spots him, runs in and stabs him to death before anyone can react. But the soldiers manning the biscuit box barricade on the far side of the yard can now see the escapees coming through the window and take aim to give them covering fire. One of them gets off a shot and brings down the Zulu who killed Hunter before he can run back into cover. The other patients have a long drop to the ground outside and most of them receive further minor injuries, but miraculously they nearly all manage to crawl across the yard and are helped over the boxes into the British position, followed by Hook and Williams.[44] Only one, Sergeant Maxfield, fails to get out. He is delirious with fever and resists all attempts to move him. The two Joneses take advantage of a pause in the enemy's attacks to run for the window, but a group of Zulus follows them, and when Robert Jones looks round for Maxfield he sees that they have surrounded his bed and are stabbing him to death.[45] He and William Jones drop into the courtyard and run for safety. Behind them part of the burning roof collapses, and the distracted Zulus do not pursue them.

Lord Chelmsford orders his column to bivouac for the night on the nek between Isandlwana and Mahlabamkhosi Hills. It is not quite dark enough to prevent the men seeing the evidence of the horrific fate of their comrades; they are forced to bivouac among heaps of dead, both British and Zulu. At least two and a half thousand men, African and British, are lying dead on the field. Somewhere among them is Colonel Degacher's younger brother William. The newcomers remain in their battle formation and carefully post sentries, fearful of a Zulu night attack. Some men are so exhausted that they lie down unawares in pools of blood.[46] Nevertheless their hunger forces them to send foragers into what remains of the camp, where they uncover a few unopened tins of bully beef. George Hamilton Browne's batman even manages to find a bottle of brandy and one of port, which are shared among the officers.[47] Soldiers often cultivate, as a survival mechanism, a feigned callousness which outsiders find hard to understand. The battlefield of Isandlwana must surely have tested this sangfroid to its very limits. Yet Browne and his comrades somehow settle down to enjoy their port and tobacco among the reeking dead. While smoking his pipe, Browne notices flashes of light in the distance around Shiyane Hill, then he sees flames leap into the sky. 'By God, the Zulus are in Natal!' one officer realises; 'Lord help the women and children!'*

---

* The casualties at Isandlwana are not known precisely, but they included nearly 800 British regulars, officers and men, plus 130 white colonial troops and around 350 of the NNC. The Zulus' mopping up was exceptionally thorough, as not one

7:40 p.m. Back at Rorke's Drift the defenders are now all inside the new defence line, abandoning the blazing hospital to the Zulus. The reduced perimeter is much easier to defend, but it has one very vulnerable point. The corner on the right of the biscuit-box barricade, where it joins the line of mealie bags along the north side of the post, is exposed to enfilading fire from three directions. The Zulus, realising this, combine long range sniping with a series of charges at this vital spot. Bromhead, Hitch and five other soldiers are now holding it. Within a few minutes the other five men are all hit, but Hitch and his officer seem to lead charmed lives.[48] The range is so short that Bromhead is doing tremendous execution with his revolver, but one Zulu manages to get over the barricade and rushes at him with his assegai. Hitch spots him and quickly takes aim at him with his rifle; this is a desperate bluff as the weapon is unloaded, but the Zulu does not know this, and instead of pressing his advantage he dives for cover on the far side of the row of boxes.

Then Frederick Hitch's luck finally runs out. He is dealing with a man to his front when he sees out of the corner of his eye a Zulu with his musket pointing at him. He tries to take aim and manages to get his Martini as far as the present position, ready to shoot, when a bullet strikes him in the right shoulder. The shoulder blade is shattered and Hitch falls to the ground, bleeding badly. Bromhead tells him 'Mate, I am very sorry to see you down,'[49] but Hitch is not down for long. He strips off his jacket and ties his useless right arm under his waist belt. He cannot hold a rifle, but Bromhead lends him his revolver and helps him to load it.

---

of Pulleine's men was found alive on the field afterwards. This may have been partly attributable to the customs of *hlomula* and *qaqa*, which would have prevented anyone from escaping by playing dead. Ian Knight has estimated that the Zulu dead must have numbered at least 1,000, mostly caused by rifle fire before they reached the camp, and that the victors may have lost almost as many as their opponents. Zulu medical services were very rudimentary, and many of their seriously wounded were probably left on the field where they would have perished from shock or loss of blood. Others were evacuated but died later from similar causes or from infection.

Alfred Hook has taken up a new position near the south wall at the opposite end of the biscuit-box wall, where Corporals Lyons and Allen are also exchanging close-range fire with Zulus hiding in the vicinity of the cookhouse. A musket ball strikes Lyons on the right side of his neck and lodges near his spine. As he falls to the ground he sees that Allen has also been hit, The latter staggers away to seek medical attention for a wound in his arm, but Lyons cannot move and at first he is left for dead.[50]

7:45 p.m. Frederick Hitch has been firing the revolver with his left hand and passing out ammunition to his comrades, but he is losing a lot of blood. One of his comrades bandages his shoulder with the lining torn from Commissary Dunne's coat, which he has left nearby, but at last Hitch falls back exhausted against the biscuit boxes. In a brief lull Private George Deacon, who has been holding the line next to him, calls out, 'Fred, when it comes to the last shall I shoot you?' He must have heard the rumours from Isandlwana of the Zulus torturing the wounded, but Hitch is still not ready to give up. 'No,' he replies, 'they have very near done for me and they can finish me right out when it comes to the last.' And at that he sinks into unconsciousness.[51]

Just outside the perimeter at Hitch's corner, the rocky ledge which had previously been an obstacle to the Zulus is now providing shelter for a group of them who are firing into the biscuit- box wall at dangerously close range. One of the former hospital patients, a young NNC corporal of Swiss origin named Ferdinand Schiess, is posted nearby with a rifle. He is suffering from an injured foot, made worse by a bullet wound received earlier in the fight, so that even walking is agonisingly painful. However, he is an experienced combat veteran, a former soldier in the French Army who fought in the Franco-Prussian War of 1870–1 at the age of fifteen, having lied about his age. He is also a very tall and powerfully built man. He spots the danger and decides to deal with it. He crawls out along the inside of the abandoned mealie-bag wall, then raises his head to try and get a shot. A Zulu sees him and fires at point-blank range, but his aim is high and he only knocks off

The north wall in front of the storehouse, which the Zulus attacked repeatedly but unsuccessfully after the hospital was abandoned. The slope has been graded since the battle to make it more accessible to visitors, and in the process much of the rock step which once protected this sector has disappeared, but an intact section of this step can still be seen at far right.

Schiess's hat. The corporal responds with unexpected speed and runs his man through with his bayonet, then shoots another of the enemy on the far side of the wall. A third Zulu runs up but is impaled on Schiess's bayonet before he can use his spear. The corporal then limps back to his post as if nothing has happened. But Lieutenant Chard has seen this heroic action, for which Schiess will later become the first South African citizen to receive the Victoria Cross.[52]

The wounded Corporal Lyons sees Chard standing over him and manages to call out to him for help. Chard, who until now has believed

Lyons to be dead, props him up against the barricade and fetches Surgeon Reynolds. Reynolds can see that it will be too dangerous to move the man before the bullet in his spine can be extracted, so he gives him emergency first aid and leaves him sitting up against the barricade. Lyons is in great pain and cannot move his head, so he asks Hook to move it for him every few minutes to try and relieve his agony. A growing number of helpless wounded, both British and Zulu, are now lying inside and outside the post, waiting for the long night to end.

Chapter 7:

The Night Battle

'We had an awful night of it here.'
(Gonville Bromhead to Captain Alfred Godwin-Austen, February 1879)

———— ⋖•⋗ ————

8:00 p.m. By now it is almost completely dark, and the hospital roof is burning well. This is fortunate for the defenders because the flames light up the courtyard between the hospital and the biscuit-box line and make it impossible for the Zulus to approach unseen. However, the glow can be seen from a great distance in the clear night. At Isandlwana, the troops camped on the battlefield can see it clearly.[1] They take it as an indication that the post at Rorke's Drift has already fallen, intensifying their mood of despair. In any case it is impossible to march to its relief in the dark, especially since in their traumatised state Chelmsford's troops believe the countryside to be swarming with Zulus.

Major Spalding, still on the road from Helpmekaar, also sees the flames. He has already been told by a series of deserters encountered on the way that the mission station has been overrun, so he takes three mounted men with him and canters ahead of the marching infantry to reconnoitre.[2] As they ride down the long slope from the Biggarsberg Mountains towards the Mzinyathi River they can see the shadowy shapes of warriors blocking the route ahead. In fact they are more of the NNC fugitives escaping from Zululand, but Spalding cannot be certain that they are not Zulus waiting in ambush. If they attack D and G Companies from close range in the dark the British rifle fire will be ineffective, and there could easily be another massacre. He decides that he is not justified in risking the lives of the men following behind him, and with a heavy heart he rejoins Upcher and Rainforth.

Gunner Howard, still hiding outside the north wall of the mission station, has somehow managed to escape detection. He is lucky because his dark blue artilleryman's overalls are less conspicuous in the dark than the red jackets of the infantry, but he is worried that the red stripes down his trouser legs will give him away. A stray pig starts squealing nearby and attracts a group of Zulus, but they still do not notice Howard next to the heap of dead horses.[3] Not far away is Private Beckett, taking cover in a ditch. He also avoids being spotted by the Zulus, but he is steadily losing blood from his stomach wound.

Inside the perimeter an extraordinary rumour is spreading. Some of the men claim to be able to see red-coated soldiers coming along the road from Helpmekaar.[4] Perhaps the movement of the two companies following Spalding is indeed discernible despite the darkness, or perhaps the flames are reflected briefly from their weapons and metal accoutrements, but when Chard is informed and peers anxiously into the night, he can see nothing. Nevertheless, a cheer goes up at the prospect of relief, and the Zulus, unsure of what it portends, briefly pause in their attacks. Two miles up the road, Spalding and the others cannot hear either the cheering or the temporarily lull in the firing from the beleaguered post. A brief discussion ensues, and then the officers give the order to turn about and return to Helpmekaar.[5] After a few moments, when the cheer is not answered and no further sightings are reported on the road, the excitement dies down at Rorke's Drift. Chard concludes that the supposed relief force must have been a false alarm. The disappointment is crushing, as the defenders realise that they are now completely on their own.

8:15 p.m. By now Dunne has finished building the new redoubt, the top of which stands about eight feet above the yard, and has brought the most seriously wounded men into the cramped space inside. They include Frederick Hitch, who is by now at best semi-conscious, though as he is carried in he manages to remark to his comrades, 'Better a bullet than an assegai.' The Zulu attacks on the western side of the post are starting to peter out, but it seems that – although there is no evidence

The surprisingly compact ring of stones in front of the church/storehouse on the left of the picture marks the position of the pile of mealie bags which Walter Dunne converted into a redoubt in preparation for the final stand around 8 p.m.

Visitors often express the view that the redoubt must have been larger than is indicated here in order to find room for the wounded inside as well as the riflemen protecting them, but in fact there was not much room for anything bigger in the cramped space between the storehouse and the mealie bags along the north wall.

———————————

of any order having been given – the warriors are beginning to mass on the other side, where the defending soldiers are occupying a stone cattle enclosure, often referred to as the 'well-built kraal', just in front of Dunne's redoubt. Here the Zulus are outside the circle of light cast by the flames from the hospital roof, and can take advantage of the cover provided by a larger but more crudely built kraal situated outside the perimeter to the north-east.*

* Frederick Hitch's adventures are based on his own written account, according to which the next thing he remembered after passing out at the barricade was Bromhead introducing him to Lord Chelmsford after the post was relieved the

8:30 p.m. Most of the Zulus have now mustered at the eastern end of the post, from where they launch a succession of attacks against the cattle kraal.[6] The defenders fall back in stages over the parallel stone walls that divide the interior of the kraal, covered by fire from Dunne's redoubt. The Zulus may no longer be silhouetted against the burning hospital, but they are still visible as they scramble over the walls, and every attempt to get close to the redoubt is thwarted by rifle fire. Several warriors try to repeat their success at the hospital by setting fire to the roof of the storehouse, but none succeed, although Lieutenant Adendorff shoots one man down at the very last moment, when his torch is almost touching the thatch.*

———

next morning. Other witnesses recalled his remark about the assegai – which was surely correct, as spear thrusts to the body were usually fatal. Only three survivors appear to have been successfully treated for wounds inflicted by spears. These were Robert Jones, Alfred Hook and John Smith, and all their wounds were regarded as minor. Hitch also seems to have played a role in rescuing the patients from the burning hospital, which he (either modestly or absent-mindedly) omitted to mention. This has led to some uncertainty over the timing of the various events which he describes, and some commentators have supposed that he received his wound before moving the patients, but this scarcely seems possible in view of the severe damage to his shoulder.

* Accounts of this phase of the battle often give the impression that the Zulus were somehow being directed by remote control. The problem is that we have no precise information about Prince Dabulamanzi's whereabouts at this stage, nor about what orders he might have issued. If he was still on Shiyane Hill he can have had little influence on events at the eastern end of the post after nightfall. We do know, from the example of Isandlwana, that Zulu units were capable of operating effectively in emergencies without any centralised control, following their traditional doctrine of encirclement and close combat. It is therefore likely that, after the initial clashes, the attacks on the defences at Rorke's Drift were organised locally by junior officers or even carried out by the men on their own initiative. I assume here that Dabulamanzi had no way of keeping informed of developments around the perimeter after about 7 p.m., nor of communicating his orders regarding troop deployments and the timing of attacks. He therefore made a virtue of necessity and allowed his subordinates to direct the battle as they saw fit in their own sectors.

The well-built cattle kraal at the eastern end of the defences, scene of the last Zulu attacks in the late evening of 22 January, viewed from the vicinity of the mealie-bag redoubt outside the storehouse. The stone walls would likely have been significantly higher in 1879 but probably still too low to give the attackers much cover from men firing down from an elevated position on top of the redoubt.

9:30 p.m. The Zulu attacks seem to be petering out, although heavy if inaccurate fire continues to pour into the post from all directions. Walter Dunne can plainly hear the Zulu officers giving commands, but frustratingly he cannot understand what they are saying.[7] Chard hears shouts of '*Usuthu!*' coming from several points, and suspects that this is being orchestrated in an attempt to confuse the defenders about the direction of the next assault.[8] After each rush is halted in front of Dunne's redoubt the Zulus retire and engage in bouts of singing and dancing to screw up their courage for the next attack. Alfred Hook believes that he can feel the ground shake under their stamping feet. Then they come again and are shot down. By now the defenders have lost count of the number of attacks they have broken up, but both casualties and exhaustion are mounting for both sides.

10:00 p.m. Somehow the Zulu *izinduna* have rallied their warriors yet again, and they send them forward in a last all-out charge, more serious than anything they have managed for the last two hours. Harry Lugg is shocked by the 'tremendous force' of the attack, and the British are finally forced to evacuate the cattle kraal and fall back into the yard next to the storehouse.[9] Then by sheer luck – or, as Lugg believes, the favour of Providence – the flames from the hospital roof flare up again and bathe the scene in sudden light. The riflemen take advantage of this to fire as fast as their fouled weapons will allow, and the Zulus are once again forced to take cover behind the walls of the kraal, leaving scores of their dead behind.

10:15 p.m. The singing and dancing stops. There are no more massed charges, just an occasional exchange of shots as the flames briefly illuminate targets on various parts of the perimeter.

At Isandlwana, Chelmsford's men are enduring a dreadful night amongst the corpses. Their commander, having learned a belated lesson in the dangers of underestimating his enemy, is up and about most of the night, checking on the sentries in case of a surprise attack. But there is no sign of the Zulus.

12 midnight. Gradually the sporadic firing at Rorke's Drift dies away. The men inside the perimeter, and especially the wounded, are by now desperately thirsty. The garrison's water cart is positioned outside the hospital and has been out of reach since the withdrawal to the biscuit-box barricade five hours ago. Now that the flames from the hospital roof are beginning to die down Bromhead, Hook and a handful of others make a sortie to retrieve it. Bromhead covers the men with his rifle while they drag the cart up to the barricade and run out the hose attached to it to enable the men on the other side to get at the precious water, but to their surprise the Zulus do not react.[10] The success of this mission is a hopeful sign that the enemy are losing heart and retreating into cover, rather than preparing to resume the assault.

Spalding, Upcher and Rainforth finally arrive back at Helpmekaar.[11] They and their men are exhausted, having been on the march most of the day without food, and they have been held up by a supply wagon which broke down on the long haul back up the mountain. On either side of the route they have seen houses and kraals in flames, apparently burnt by Zulu raiding parties. They consider themselves lucky to have survived the disaster which they believe has overwhelmed their comrades at Rorke's Drift. Edward Essex and the remaining men at Helpmekaar are equally jumpy, and there is a brief moment of consternation when they mistake their returning comrades for a Zulu *impi*. But at the last minute they recognise the British uniforms and a friendly-fire incident is averted.

Chapter 8

23 January

'An awful time of suspense.' *(Henry Hook)*

———◦•◦———

4:00 a.m. It has been quiet for the last few hours at Rorke's Drift, with just occasional shots being fired by nervous lookouts on both sides. Most of the Zulus have been taking cover among the rocks and bushes around the post, but now they begin a gradual withdrawal, anxious to reach safety before daylight reveals them to the defenders. Those wounded who can walk, or whose comrades manage to help them, go with them, but they leave behind them hundreds of dead and seriously wounded warriors scattered on the ground all around the perimeter.[1]

5:00 a.m. Lord Chelmsford is anxious to leave the battlefield at Isandlwana before daylight reveals the full extent of the disaster and demoralises his troops even further. As the 'time of the horns' approaches he rouses them and prepares to march to Rorke's Drift. Hamilton Browne goes in search of his tent in the hope that he might be able to salvage a few of his belongings. On his way across the battlefield he sees some terrible sights: mutilated bodies of British infantrymen lying about in groups of two or three, surrounded by dead Zulus.[2] When he reaches his tent he finds his African groom, two horses and his setter dog, all dead from spear wounds. Nearby are two of his officers, also dead, with piles of empty cartridges beside them. He also sees hundreds of Zulu corpses, and has time to reflect on the courage of the enemy in pressing the attack home despite such losses. Then the bugle sounds, and he is obliged to hurry back to his post without having had time to dismount. On the way back he stops his horse suddenly, spotting in front of him the body of Henry Pulleine. There is nothing he can do but salute his old friend and carry on.

As the first light of dawn appears in the sky at Rorke's Drift, John Waters stands up and sees to his enormous relief that the mealie bags are still manned by red-coated soldiers. He walks up to the perimeter – lucky not to be shot by a nervous defender, as he is still wearing Otto Witt's black cloak – and is helped inside to have his wounded shoulder dressed.[3] Men begin to climb over the barricades and cautiously examine the dead and wounded Zulus who are still lying where they fell last night. Chard notes the appalling wounds inflicted on them at close range by the Martini Henry bullets – skulls shattered, and heads split apart as though with an axe. Private Beckett is found in a ditch, too weak to get up, and is carried in by his comrades, but he dies soon afterwards from loss of blood. Chard's mule driver comes in, traumatised by his experience in the cave on the hill. A single Zulu, who has been taking cover in the cattle kraal, also takes advantage of the growing daylight. He leaps to his feet, fires a single defiant shot from his musket at the men on the barricade, and then runs in the direction of the river. Several men shoot at him as he goes, but he is not hit and makes his escape successfully. Chard admires the 'plucky fellow', and for once is glad to see his men miss their target. Another African is brought in alive, and claims to be a survivor of the NNC who has somehow made his way there from Isandlwana. Chard is sceptical, and summons Daniels the ferryman to interrogate him in isiZulu. Daniels does so with the aid of Major Spalding's sword, which he flourishes so enthusiastically that the man fears for his life. But his story seems convincing, so Chard lets him go with a message to the commander at Helpmekaar, asking him to send help urgently.*

5:30 a.m. Chelmsford's column begins its despondent march past the looming height of Isandlwana, picking its way gingerly over a carpet of corpses, and back towards Rorke's Drift.

---

* No one seems to have recorded what Daniels was doing all night, and as a civilian he was not necessarily expected to help hold the perimeter, but he was clearly a brave and resourceful individual, and his offer to defend the ponts implies that he knew how to use a rifle. His contribution to the defence may therefore have been greater than is commonly recognised.

7:00 a.m. At the mission station the garrison's spirits suddenly sink again as a large group of Zulus is spotted on the low hill north-west of the post, on the far side of the Helpmekaar road.[4] Chard orders the men outside the perimeter to come in at once, and they take up their positions again with rifles at the ready. The infantrymen still have plenty of ammunition in their pouches, but Chard knows that once this is expended there is only a box and a half left in reserve. If the attack is renewed they will not be able to resist for long. But the enemy do not advance; there are some mysterious comings and goings between the hill and the flank of Shiyane, but most of the warriors remain squatting in the grass.

Lord Chelmsford's column is coming up from the valley of the Manzimnyama and climbing the rise which separates it from the Mzinyathi, when they begin to see bands of Zulus coming towards them from the direction of Rorke's Drift. Soon there are thousands of the enemy in sight, travelling in groups on either side of the road.[5] Lieutenant Harford believes that they are marching into an ambush, and gallops to the head of the column to alert the general in case he has somehow not seen them. But Chelmsford orders the men to keep marching, and only to respond if the Zulus attack. In fact, neither side wants to initiate a fight. The British are exhausted physically and mentally after their traumatic night; they are strung out in a long column which it will be very difficult to redeploy into battle formation, and they have almost no ammunition. The Zulus have been fighting all night and are scarcely any less exhausted. They have also had a recent lesson in the damage that the British soldiers can inflict. What is more, they left Isandlwana yesterday believing that Chelmsford's army had been utterly destroyed, so they cannot understand where these new enemies have come from. Certainly, they have no reason to doubt that they are fresh and fully supplied.

7:15 a.m. The armies pass each other travelling in opposite directions at a distance of no more than 300 yards. They watch each other mostly in silence, although some of Chelmsford's NNC are bold enough to call

Looking north-west across the Helpmekaar road from a viewpoint near the river crossing at Rorke's Drift. At about 7 a.m. on 23 January a large body of Zulus occupied this ridge and observed the post for approximately an hour before moving off. Although the defenders feared that they might be fresh troops preparing for another attack, they were in fact part of Dabulamanzi's defeated army resting and rallying prior to leaving.

out to the uThulwana, asking them where they have come from. One of the uThulwana warriors has the impression that the NNC want to fight, but their officers forbid it.[6] On a ridge overlooking the road a group of Zulus squats down to watch the enemy procession, but then one of them suddenly leaps to his feet and tries to incite his comrades to charge. The others ignore him, so he rushes down the hill towards the British column. No one is sure what he intends to do, but neither does anyone want to take a chance. When he gets to within thirty yards one of the soldiers shoots him dead. Both sides then resume their march, leaving the lone hero's body where it has fallen.[7]

8:00 a.m. The Zulus on the hill overlooking the mission station suddenly stand up and walk slowly away out of sight. From their position they can see – as Chard and his men still cannot – Chelmsford's column approaching the drift over the Mzinyathi River and preparing to cross over.[8]

8:05 a.m. Chelmsford still does not know whether the post has held out, but he fears the worst. So too do Chard's men, who can now see the NNC troops at the head of the relief column, but mistake them for Zulu reinforcements. With tensions reaching an unbearable level on both sides, Chelmsford sends his Mounted Infantry ahead to determine whether any of the defenders might still be alive.

8:15 a.m. The column from Isandlwana is still strung out crossing the river, but its commander is already across, impatient for news. Henry Harford, accompanying Chelmsford, is one of several officers who raise their field glasses and strain their eyes for any signs of survivors among the buildings as they approach. Then suddenly they see a figure standing on the hospital roof and waving a flag. As he is recognised as a British soldier a loud cheer breaks out, followed soon afterwards by an answering cheer from the post.[9] Major Cecil Russell and Lieutenant Walsh, at the head of the Mounted Infantry, have arrived at the barricades, followed moments later by the commander-in-chief himself. Their first question, after the noise has died down, is whether any survivors of the 1st Battalion have managed to escape from Isandlwana and join the defenders. On learning from Walter Dunne that they have not, one of the officers cannot restrain his sobs of grief.[10]

Others in the relief column have more pragmatic concerns, for they are extremely hungry and Rorke's Drift still has supplies of food. The wounded Dalton is somehow able not only to walk but to take charge of issuing rations. George Hamilton Browne enjoys bully beef and biscuits, eaten with his fingers for lack of plates or cutlery, then makes

Looking north-west from the upper slopes of Shiyane, up the Mzinyathi Valley. The crossing at Rorke's Drift is marked by the modern bridge in the middle distance. The mission station is partly hidden by the hill at far left. Lord Chelmsford's column reached the drift at around 8:15 on 23 January, having passed the retreating Zulus travelling in the opposite direction.

tea in the empty beef tins. Tea is also Hook's priority, and he is brewing up in the cookhouse in his shirt sleeves when a sergeant arrives and summons him to meet Lord Chelmsford.[11] He is reluctant to appear in front of his superiors until he is properly dressed, but the NCO is insistent, so he stands uncomfortably without his jacket and with his braces hanging loose while he briefs the general about the defence of the hospital. An officer whom he does not know takes his name and that of several other men, and makes notes about what they have done. Chard's first thought is to wash his face, although the only place to do so is a muddy puddle which he shares with Private Bushe, who is trying to clean up a nasty wound to his nose. Bushe lends him half of his filthy towel, and feeling slightly more presentable the lieutenant goes to greet the commander-in-chief, who congratulates him on the gallant defence.[12] Then Chard wanders over to inspect his wagon. This has been left outside the perimeter all night with its miscellaneous contents, and the enemy have wrecked and looted it despite the attempts of his batman, Driver Robson, to drive them away from it with rifle fire. But all is not quite lost, because the Zulus have inexplicably missed an unopened bottle of beer. Chard shares this with Bromhead, in the midst of the wreckage and the corpses, 'with mutual congratulations on having come safely out of so much danger'.*

* The generally accepted total of defenders who were killed at Rorke's Drift or died of wounds afterwards, including the patients in the hospital, is seventeen. The Zulu dead numbered at least 350, and possibly many more.

Chapter 9

The Aftermath

'I have not got over the wonder of there being one of
us left.' *(Gonville Bromhead to his sister, February 1879)*

The immediate result of the defeat at Isandlwana was that what was
left of Number Three Column fell back across the border into Natal,
and the forward momentum of the entire British invasion faltered.[1]
Cetshwayo saw clearly that the victory had brought only a temporary
respite, and he never fully forgave either Ntshingwayo or Dabulamanzi
for the losses they had incurred. After 22 January the Zulus never
achieved another comparable success. They inflicted defeats on British
forces in March at Intombe Drift and Hlobane, and in June hit the
headlines again when they killed the Prince Imperial of France, Louis
Bonaparte, the last in the dynasty founded by the great Napoleon,
who was accompanying Lord Chelmsford in an unofficial capacity.
But by the end of March Chelmsford was receiving reinforcements
from Britain and resuming the offensive, while the Zulus never fully
recovered from their losses. On 29 March an *impi* attacked Colonel
Wood's Number Four column at Khambula. Among them were the
iNgobamakhosi, uMbonambi and uKhandempemvu regiments, who
advanced shouting 'We are the boys from Isandlwana!' But Wood's
men were in a strong defensive position and the Zulus were repulsed
with the loss of around 2,000 men, compared to 18 British killed. At
Gingindhlovu on 2 April Chelmsford himself won a similar victory,
having learned his lesson and deployed within the protection of a
wagon *laager*. On 21 May a British force returned to Isandlwana and
began the grisly task of identifying and burying the dead. Finally, on
4 July, Chelmsford's new army, strengthened by the addition of Gatling

machine guns and two units of regular cavalry, brought Cetshwayo's last army to battle on the plain outside his *ikhanda* at oNdini. In this encounter, known to the British as the Battle of Ulundi, Chelmsford's men formed a single large square from which they shot down every Zulu who got close to them, then released the cavalry on the wavering enemy. In the aftermath oNdini was sacked and the king fled. The war was over, but there was to be no peace for Zululand. Years of civil strife, encouraged by the British policy of sharing power among no fewer than thirteen puppet chiefs and exacerbated by Boer incursions, reduced the kingdom to such a state that the British felt obliged to annex it in the interests of regional stability. In 1897 it was absorbed into Natal. The Zulus were not to regain their freedom for nearly a century, until the establishment of a democratic South Africa in the 1990s.

The *inkatha yesizwe* was taken back to its home at esiKlebhene, near the grave of Shaka's father Senzangakhona, where it was unwittingly burnt in a hut by a British cavalry patrol in June 1879. Some of King Cetshwayo's subjects believed that his failure to observe the proper ceremonies regarding the sacred rope was a factor in the high Zulu casualties at Isandlwana. The king was captured in August and imprisoned at Cape Town, but after a visit to London in 1881, when he was greeted by cheering crowds who admired the way he had fought to defend his kingdom, he was allowed to return home. Unfortunately he was restored only to part of his former territory, while his rivals, notably Zibhebhu kaMaphitha, who had now turned against his king, were allowed to retain their new possessions. The result was civil war, in which Cetshwayo's faction, the Usuthu, was defeated by Zibhebhu at the Battles of oNdini and Msebe in 1883. Cetshwayo escaped and sought British protection, but in February 1884 he died at Eshowe in mysterious circumstances. He may have suffered a heart attack, but many of his supporters believed that Zibhebhu had ordered him to be poisoned.

Ntshingwayo kaMahole, the victor of Isandlwana, did not receive the rewards he deserved from Cetshwayo as he was blamed by rival *izinduna* for attacking without orders, and for the heavy casualties

This memorial to the Zulu dead at Isandlwana was belatedly erected in 1999.
It utilises the symbolism of the *'isiqu'* necklace, the highest Zulu award for bravery,
and the traditional headrest, alluding to the spirits of men now resting in peace.
Amatutshane is at far left, and the hills around Mangeni are partly hidden by cloud
in the distance.

which his army had suffered. After the war he was one of the thirteen
puppet chiefs set up by the British to replace the king's authority.
Nevertheless, he remained loyal to Cetshwayo, and fought in his
defence against Zibhebhu at the Battle of oNdini. There the royal army
was routed, and Ntshingwayo was overtaken and killed as he tried to
escape.[2]

Cetshwayo was similarly displeased with Prince Dabulamanzi's dis-
obedience in invading Natal, but his career was only briefly affected,
and he was one of the commanders at the siege of Fort Eshowe and

A buffalo thorn tree at Isandlwana. These trees are traditionally planted to mark the place where a Zulu has died away from home.

the subsequent Battle of Gingindhlovu on 2 April 1879, where he was wounded. After the war he supported Cetshwayo against Zibhebhu, but was again defeated at the Battle of Msebe. In 1886 he was murdered by a Boer who had wrongly accused him of stock theft.

Mehlokazulu kaSihayo was arrested by the British after the war because of his involvement in the raid into Natal in search of his father's errant wives, which had helped to precipitate the conflict. However, he argued that he had only acted under orders from the king, and was eventually released. He was killed fighting against the British once again in the Bambatha Rebellion of 1906.

In Britain the defeat at Isandlwana was a personal blow to Benjamin Disraeli, who had been Conservative Prime Minister since 1874. In

April 1880 he was defeated in a general election by the Liberal Party under William Gladstone, and although issues such as the agricultural depression were dominant in the campaign, Gladstone also scored points by criticising his opponent's foreign policy failures in South Africa and elsewhere. Disraeli died a year later.

Sir Bartle Frere was officially censured for his role in provoking and mismanaging the war, but Disraeli at first allowed him to remain in his post. However, his dream of Confederation was in tatters, and after the 1880 election he was recalled and charged with misconduct. He died four years later, still fighting to clear his name.

In the wake of the Isandlwana disaster Sir Garnet Wolseley was sent out to replace Lord Chelmsford, but the latter managed to secure his victory at Ulundi before his successor could arrive at the front, thus partially redeeming his reputation. He and his supporters attempted to pass the blame for the defeat on to others, primarily Colonels Glyn and Durnford and the African troops of the NNC, and in this Chelmsford had the support of Queen Victoria. The War Office, however, was not fooled, and in August 1879 announced the conclusion that the main cause of the disaster was 'the under estimate formed of the offensive fighting power of the Zulu army'. The implication, clearly, was that this was the responsibility of the commander-in-chief. Chelmsford was effectively 'kicked upstairs'. He was confirmed in his rank of lieutenant-general and subsequently held the prestigious positions of governor of the Tower of London and colonel of the Life Guards, but the government made sure that he was never again entrusted with the lives of troops in the field. He died in 1905 at the age of seventy-seven.[3]

Richard Glyn suffered from depression after the events of 22 January, but his career survived the determined attempts by Chelmsford to blame him for the disaster which had befallen his battalion while he was not in command of it. He led a brigade in the Ulundi campaign, and later returned to the 1st/24th. He ended up as a lieutenant-general, and in 1898 was appointed to the honorary position of colonel of the South Wales Borderers, the successors of the old 24th Foot. He died two years later.

Anthony Durnford's story did not end with his death on the field of Isandlwana, and the controversy over his responsibility for the events which led to his death has continued to the present day. Colonel Crealock opened the debate by asserting that the orders which he issued to Durnford on the morning of 22 January included an instruction to take command of the camp on his arrival there. The implication was that Durnford had been negligent in disregarding this and continuing his advance beyond the camp. Unfortunately for Crealock the orders later turned up and were found to contain no such instruction. To be charitable to Crealock, he may not have kept a copy of the orders and later assumed that the issue of command had been covered, as with hindsight it certainly should have been. Durnford's own family mounted a strong defence of his reputation, supported by his friend Bishop Colenso, and he was eventually buried with due ceremony in the military cemetery in Pietermaritzburg.

George Hamilton Browne's later life was as colourful as it had always been. He was at the Battle of Gingindhlovu in April 1879, and continued to raise and command various bodies of irregular troops in South Africa. His last campaign was the Matabele War of 1893. In 1908 he applied for a pension on account of his service in New Zealand, but this was refused as no proof could be found that he had actually seen action against the Maoris there, as he claimed. Instead he married a rich heiress, squandered her fortune and retired to Jamaica, where he died in 1913.

Only five British regular army officers escaped from Isandlwana: Henry Curling, Edward Essex, Alan Gardner, Horace Smith-Dorrien and William Cochrane. All of them gave evidence at the Court of Inquiry which Chelmsford held after the battle, but none had been involved in the command decisions under investigation. Of these Curling was the only one who had actually fought on the front line and survived. He wrote a series of letters from Zululand, which were eventually published in 2001 (*The Curling Letters of the Zulu War*, eds. Greaves & Best) He went on to serve in Afghanistan, and in 1895 was promoted to lieutenant-colonel in command of the Royal Artillery in Egypt. He died in Ramsgate in 1910 at the age of sixty-four.

Edward Essex fought at Ulundi and his sword, which he had left in his tent before the fighting began at Isandlwana, was found among the weapons surrendered by the Zulus after the victory. He went on to serve in the First Anglo-Boer War and also survived the battles of Laing's Nek and Ingogo. Not surprisingly, he was known to his contemporaries as 'lucky Essex'. He became an instructor at Sandhurst and finished his career as a colonel commanding the Gordon Highlanders, into which his old regiment had been amalgamated in 1881.

Horace Smith-Dorrien had to walk all the way to Helpmekaar, but recovered and went on to a very successful career, serving in Egypt and India, and commanding a Sudanese battalion at the Battle of Omdurman in 1898. He was mentioned in dispatches for his performance in the Boer War of 1899–1902, and was promoted to lieutenant-general in 1906. In the following year he took over as GOC at Aldershot and introduced numerous reforms in the training of the army, especially concerning marksmanship. He became a full general in 1912, and on the outbreak of the First World War he commanded II Corps of the British Expeditionary Force in France. He earned the displeasure of his commander, Sir John French, by disobeying an order to retreat at Le Cateau on 26 August 1914. Many later believed that his decision to stand and fight saved the BEF from destruction, but French's hostility eventually led to his dismissal. He was governor of Gibraltar from 1918 to 1923, and published his memoirs in 1925. He was killed in a car accident in 1930, at the age of seventy-two.

Alan Gardner also reached safety at Helpmekaar, but then set out on an arduous ride to take the news of Isandlwana to Evelyn Wood's Number Four Column, which was thirty miles away near Ncome . On account of this he was considered for the VC, but was turned down on the grounds that, although a notable feat of endurance, his journey had not been sufficiently dangerous. He had a horse killed under him at the Battle of Hlobane and was wounded at Kambula, but survived the war and resigned from the army two years later. He and his wife later became minor celebrities as big-game hunters. Gardner was elected as a Liberal Member of Parliament in 1906, but died in the following year.

William Cochrane also went on to fight at Hlobane and Kambula, and in Kitchener's 1898 campaign in the Sudan, He died in 1927 as a brigadier-general. The same year also saw the death of Henry Harford, who had risen to command a battalion of his regiment, the 99th Foot, retired early on medical grounds, but survived to the age of eighty-six. In the aftermath of Isandlwana Harford had found himself in the embarrassing situation of having to take charge of two fellow officers who were under arrest for desertion – Walter Higginson and William Stevenson. Later, however, he was responsible for a more distinguished prisoner, King Cetshwayo himself, of whom he left an admiring description.

Lieutenants Melvill and Coghill have been celebrated as heroes ever since the battle, despite occasional doubts as to whether the former was really ordered to take the Queen's Colour to safety or simply saw an opportunity to escape with his own life. Their bodies were found where they had fallen by a patrol on 3 February, and the following day Henry Harford, accompanying a burial party, discovered the lost flag in the river, whose level had dropped considerably since the battle. The colour was taken back to Rorke's Drift where it was presented to Colonel Glyn. The grave and a memorial to the two officers still overlook Fugitives' Drift. It was widely considered at the time that they both deserved the VC, but the regulations did not then permit it to be awarded posthumously. This was rectified in 1907 after the rules were changed.

Simeon Nkambule was promoted to sergeant-major and served at the battles of Hlobane, Kambula and Ulundi. He was awarded the Distinguished Conduct Medal, but the Reverend Owen Watkins believed with good reason that 'Had he been a white man, he would have received the Victoria Cross.'

Trooper Barker was recommended for the VC for giving up his horse to Lieutenant Higginson after the crossing of the Mzinyathi, but the request was turned down by the War Office.

Troopers Dorehill and Hayes got safely away from Fugitives' Drift, but Hayes died of fever at Helpmekaar a month later. Dorehill

The well-tended grave of Lieutenants Melvill and Coghill overlooking the
Mzinyathi River. Their story has always captured the imagination of the British,
and a regular flow of VIP visitors to the grave attests to its continuing appeal.

eventually discovered the identity of the elderly African who had saved
his life by shooting his assailants on the bank of the river. He was an
employee of the Natal magistrate Henry Fynn named Jacob, who had
escaped from Isandlwana by taking off the red cloth that distinguished
the NNC troops and disguising himself as a Zulu. He not only got
away but managed to recover Dorehill's carbine, which he had dropped
when he jumped into the river, and returned it to him.[4]

By May a new fort, known as Fort Melvill, had been built to defend
the river crossing at Rorke's Drift, but until then the wrecked buildings
and all pervasive mud at the mission station made it a particularly

unpleasant posting, although the veterans of the fight enjoyed the rare luxury of a tarpaulin to sleep under. In the aftermath of the battle John Chard appears to have suffered from some degree of post-traumatic stress, or at least from severe exhaustion. This is not surprising: on 22 January he had made the return trip from Rorke's Drift to Isandlwana on horseback – which today tourists regard as a full-day excursion – then continued with his work on the ponts until interrupted by news of the approaching Zulus, oversaw the construction of the defences, and finally fought a hand-to-hand battle of unprecedented ferocity which lasted for most of the following night. As commander of the post he would not have been able to snatch even a moment's rest. One unsympathetic observer remarked that subsequently, instead of taking advantage of his fame to seek advancement, he 'smokes his pipe and says nothing',[5] but he was nevertheless awarded the Victoria Cross and promoted to major. He received an audience with Queen Victoria, for whom he wrote a detailed report on the fight at Rorke's Drift. He remained in the Royal Engineers and ended up as a colonel. Ironically, it would be his iconic pipe that would eventually kill him; he developed cancer of the tongue and died, aged only forty-nine, in 1897.

Gonville Bromhead also received the VC and a brevet promotion to major, but unluckily missed out on his invitation to meet the Queen as he was on leave when it arrived. He stayed in the army and died of fever at Allahabad, India, in 1891. James Reynolds was also awarded the VC for his conduct on 22 January. He reached the rank of surgeon lieutenant-colonel, retired in 1896 and lived in London until his death in 1932.

It took a while for Commissary James Dalton's contribution to be properly recognised, perhaps because he left for six months' sick leave after being wounded at Rorke's Drift, but he eventually received his VC in November 1879. He became something of a drifter, going home to England then returning to South Africa to prospect for gold. He died suddenly in Port Elizabeth of unknown causes in 1887. His colleague Walter Dunne went on to see action in the First Anglo-Boer War of

1881, at Tel el-Kebir and in the Sudan. He was not awarded the VC, for reasons that are still controversial, but did eventually end up as a Companion of the Bath. He retired due to ill health in 1908, and died in Rome later that year at the age of fifty-five.

As a civilian the Reverend George Smith was not eligible for a medal for his gallantry at Rorke's Drift, but he was instead commissioned as a regular army chaplain. He was known for the rest of his life as 'Ammunition Smith' for his role in supplying the fighting men during the battle. He served at the Battle of Tel el-Kebir in Egypt in 1882, and at several other battles in the Sudan, and died in 1918.

Frederick Hitch's wound was serious – he was told that thirty-eight fragments of shattered bone were eventually removed from his shoulder – but with the aid of Bromhead's nursing he recovered, although he was invalided out of the army. While in hospital at Netley near Southampton he received his Victoria Cross from none other than the Queen herself, who recorded that he was quite speechless and afterwards fainted.[6] He produced several accounts of his experiences at Rorke's Drift, differing in minor details. Hitch later worked as a taxi driver, and died in London in 1913, at the age of fifty-six.

Alfred Hook left the army in 1880 but later served part time in the 1st Volunteer Battalion, Royal Fusiliers. Thanks to the support of Chelmsford and Bromhead he got a job as a cloakroom attendant at the British Museum. The apparently minor scalp wound he had received at Rorke's Drift continued to cause him pain in later life. He retired to Gloucestershire where he died of tuberculosis in 1905, aged fifty-four.

Towards the end of 1936 a medium not even imagined in 1879, the BBC Regional Radio Service, broadcast a series of programmes with the title 'I Was There'. Along with other famous survivors like Charles Lightoller, who had been Second Officer on the *Titanic*, the BBC interviewed Lieutenant-Colonel Frank Bourne, OBE, DCM – the 'kid' himself, now in his eighties, and as far as he knew the only one of the Rorke's Drift defenders still alive. Bourne was another veteran whom many thought had been unjustly omitted from the list of those who deserved the Victoria Cross. He was offered a commission after the battle, but was unable to accept it as he lacked the private income which was required to maintain an officer's lifestyle in those days. Later he became a quartermaster with honorary commissioned rank, served as adjutant to a school of musketry in the First World War, and ended his career in 1918 as a lieutenant-colonel. He died in Kent in 1945 at the age of ninety-one. BBC archivists subsequently destroyed the tape of his radio broadcast, but – allowing for the occasional confusion over details due to the lapse of time – the transcript remains a valuable source for the events of 22 January.[7]

Neither of the two Joneses, William and Robert, who had so valiantly defended the hospital ever fully recovered from the strain of their ordeal, although both received well-earned VCs. William, who was nearly forty years old at the time of the battle, contracted rheumatism as a result of sleeping at the post in all weathers and was invalided out of the army. He went onto the stage, relating his experiences in music halls and joining Buffalo Bill's Wild West Show, but never prospered and eventually had to pawn his medal. He later suffered from dementia, and was said to be in the habit of taking his granddaughter out of the house and running into the streets, shouting that the Zulus were coming. He was admitted to the Manchester workhouse and died in 1913. Robert Jones married and worked on a farm in Herefordshire, but he began to suffer from nightmares and pains in the head, which were attributed to his experiences at Rorke's Drift. He was forty-one years old when, in 1898, he borrowed his employer's shotgun and committed suicide.

The fate of the heroic Corporal Schiess was also a tragic one. He was awarded the VC early in 1880, and emigrated to India. Subsequently he returned to South Africa but was unable to find work, and in 1884 he was discovered sick and homeless in Cape Town. The Royal Navy gave him free passage to England on a troopship, but he died during the voyage. He was only twenty-eight years old. Although he was penniless, his Victoria Cross was still in his pocket when he died.

John Williams, alias Fielding, also earned the VC. He left the army in 1883 but returned to serve in the 3rd Volunteer Battalion of the South Wales Borderers, and was a recruiting sergeant in the First World War.

The latest memorial to the Zulus at Rorke's Drift features a leopard, a symbol of military power and the source of the insignia of high-ranking *izinduna*, on a pile of shields.

He was seventy-five when he died in Cwmbran in 1932, probably the last surviving Rorke's Drift VC winner.

Otto Witt successfully escaped from Rorke's Drift, but both he and his wife were told that the other had been killed by the Zulus. They were eventually reunited when they met by chance on the road. Witt returned to his mission in 1880 and rebuilt it, but his claim for compensation was rejected by the British authorities, who ruled that the damage it had sustained was the fault of the Zulus and not of the army. He retired to Sweden in 1891 and died in 1923.

Conclusion

It is not the purpose of this account to allocate blame for the disaster which overtook British arms on 22 January, but the 'minute by minute' approach inevitably leads to the question of whether different decisions could have been made at certain specific times, potentially leading to different outcomes. The official British verdict on the defeat at Isandlwana, enshrined in the *Narrative of Field Operations* published in 1881, blamed the collapse of the line on a unit of NNC troops deployed in the centre, who had allegedly fled at the crucial moment. This is discounted by many recent scholars for two main reasons. One is the impossibility of identifying this unit and constructing a plausible route by which it could have got into that position. As we have seen, various elements of the NNC did fall back on the regulars' position in the face of the Zulu attack, but none of them was large enough to have occupied a substantial portion of the line and most of them seem to have taken up less exposed positions slightly to the rear. It also seems highly unlikely that Lieutenant-Colonel Pulleine would have ordered the NNC to deploy in the centre, because of the risk of compromising the integrity of his firing line by including in it men whose equipment and marksmanship were inferior to those of the regulars.

The real deficiency in the British deployment was the lack of any reserves. Lord Chelmsford's 'Instructions' issued to column commanders before the invasion (reproduced as an appendix in Greaves, *Isandlwana*) included a diagram of an ideal battle formation, with artillery in the centre, flanked by British infantry and with mounted troops slightly to the rear on the wings, and NNC units behind them. This is not dissimilar to the deployment that Pulleine managed to achieve, even in haste and under threat of imminent attack – with one glaring exception. Chelmsford's drawing shows a second line of regular infantry drawn up behind the first, both to reinforce the front line and to guard against it being outflanked. But, fatally, the companies that should have formed this line were not available at Isandlwana, because the commander-in-chief himself had divided his forces and led them away to Mangeni the night before.

Pulleine might perhaps have improvised a different deployment taking account of his reduced strength. He could perhaps have drawn his infantry companies together into a battalion square as soon as he realised that a serious attack was developing – around noon. Such a square had no flanks that were vulnerable to encirclement, and could perhaps have held out until Chelmsford could return to relieve it – if its ammunition had lasted. It may be appropriate here to discuss the famous British square, which is sometimes brought up as though it was the answer to every problem in colonial warfare. In the Napoleonic Wars it had been common practice to deploy single infantry battalions in square formation so that they could defend themselves against cavalry, who would otherwise use their superior mobility to envelop their flanks. With the men drawn up shoulder-to-shoulder two or three ranks deep, and with no need to worry about being taken in the rear, they could present a hedge of bayonets which it was almost impossible for horsemen to break into. The main drawbacks of the formation were its lack of mobility and its vulnerability to artillery, and the squares worked best when they were carefully positioned so that they could support each other with musketry, without being so close as to risk casualties by friendly fire.

In the colonial wars of the later nineteenth century it was more usual to employ brigade squares, in effect turning the whole army into one large square which might consist of several infantry battalions, with artillery at the corners and cavalry protected inside the square, ready to charge out when the enemy faltered. With the new longer-ranged rifles now being used by the infantry, a single large square was also safer than several small ones from the point of view of friendly fire. This was the formation which brought victory at Ulundi. The disadvantages of the square formation now applied to the whole force, but the risk was worthwhile as most lightly equipped non-European opponents, especially in Africa, lacked artillery, even if they were almost as mobile as cavalry. But by threatening their homelands, villages and cattle they could usually be persuaded to attack the British square while it was stationary. The larger the formation the more resilient it tended to be.

A brigade square could enclose supporting arms, senior officers and ammunition wagons, but Pulleine did not have this option at Isandlwana because his regular infantry force had already been reduced to the equivalent of a single battalion. Even if he had had the time to drawn up the companies which he had under his command into a square, there would not have been room inside for the wagons, oxen and stores, let alone the tents and their contents, so this would have meant in effect abandoning the camp, which he had orders to defend. It would also, of course, have meant abandoning Durnford, who could hardly have been persuaded to give up his plans to take the offensive. The remaining option, which the 1st/24th was trying to adopt when it was overrun, was to form small rallying squares from the individual companies. However, as we have seen, these were too small to survive on their own for more than a few minutes.

Other 'what ifs' might not have altered the outcome significantly. At 2 a.m. on 22 January Lord Chelmsford might have decided not to march to reinforce Dartnell, but instead to recall the latter to Isandlwana at first light. The camp would then probably not have been attacked that day, but Ntshingwayo and Mavumengwana were already in a good position to launch an offensive on the 23rd, when they might have caught the whole of Number Three Column strung out on the march. Alternatively, Chelmsford might have come back as soon as he received Hamilton Browne's first message warning him of the attack on the camp, not long after 1 p.m., but even then he could not have arrived at Isandlwana in time to affect the issue.

Perhaps Major Bengough's battalion could have made a difference if it had received timely and relevant orders, either at Isandlwana or at

Rorke's Drift, but this is pure speculation. An NNC battalion had less than a tenth of the firepower of its British equivalent because of its lack of rifles and training, and the men, who were all too well aware of this deficiency, would probably have been no more eager than their comrades in other NNC units to sacrifice themselves for Queen Victoria.

If Anthony Durnford had stayed and taken command of the camp after his arrival instead of riding off eastward, he might not have despatched the mounted troops under Raw and Roberts who accidentally triggered the Zulu attack. But someone else could easily have done; the plateau was already being criss-crossed by British patrols, some of which, sent out by Lieutenant Scott from his post on Amatutshane, did in fact sight the enemy in the vicinity of the Ngwebeni Valley at around the same time. And Durnford's force was probably not strong enough to affect the outcome of the battle even if it had remained with Pulleine: the musketry of the cavalry was inferior to that of the regulars, and the rocket battery was not much more than a gimmick. It is probably fair to say that Pulleine, with his lack of combat experience, was rather out of his depth at Isandlwana, and that Durnford was an unwelcome distraction for him, but the timings show that the latter cannot be held responsible for Pulleine's failure to concentrate his companies.

It is on the whole more instructive to think of Isandlwana not as a British defeat but as a Zulu success. Ntshingwayo's flanking manoeuvre before the battle was masterly, and even though the day itself did not go according to his plans, his regiments showed themselves capable of improvising and carrying out a battle plan in accordance with their tactical doctrine. Most important of all, the courage and determination of the Zulu warriors and their officers in the face of British firepower, which was far more deadly than anything they had ever encountered before, saw them through to victory despite their heavy losses.

As for Rorke's Drift, if Dabulamanzi had had his regiments under closer control, perhaps they might have stormed the post in one overwhelming rush while they were still relatively fresh. But the British too would have been fresh and still well-supplied with ammunition, and, despite their proverbial discipline and courage, the Zulus were only human. Their front ranks would have suffered catastrophic losses to close-range volley fire and those behind would have been advancing over heaps of corpses. Shaka might have driven them on regardless to a costly victory, but Dabulamanzi was no Shaka. Spalding, Upcher and Rainforth might have pressed on towards Rorke's Drift on the evening of 22 January instead of turning back to Helpmekaar, especially if there was no fire visible to suggest that the post had fallen. They might also have walked into an ambush in the dark; even if the figures they saw on the road were in fact friends, if the garrison at the post were aware of their approach, then so must the besieging Zulus have been.

Professor John Laband has considered the likely consequences of a Zulu victory at Rorke's Drift in his alternate history *The Fall of Rorke's Drift*. He argues that the setback to British prestige might have encouraged the Boers in the Transvaal and perhaps elsewhere to rise in revolt. This could have induced the government in London to make Cetshwayo a more lenient peace offer, including dropping the demand that the Zulu army be disbanded, but the king would still have had to accept terms which undermined his already contested authority among his own people. The Zulu civil war, the Boer interventions and the eventual loss of independence would therefore not have been prevented in the long run.

All battles are tragedies, but Isandlwana cast a longer shadow than most. The dramatic reversal of fortune for the all-conquering British; the unprecedented total annihilation of the equivalent of a whole battalion; the poignant image of the redcoat infantry facing their inevitable deaths with discipline and courage while those lucky enough to have horses rode away to safety; all these intensified the shock on the losing side. Even to the Zulus the battle was as much a disaster as a victory: Cetshwayo famously likened the loss of so many of his warriors to 'an assegai thrust into the belly of the nation', lamenting that 'there are not enough tears to mourn the dead'.

For the British the successful defence of Rorke's Drift went some way towards mitigating the shock. After the war Chelmsford's successor, Sir

Garnet Wolseley, was scathing about the glorification of the defenders, arguing that they had had no choice but to fight 'like rats in a hole', just to save their own skins. But popular feeling was against him, grateful for at least one victory to relieve the disaster of Isandlwana. In March another cartoon published in *Punch* had paid tribute to Chard and Bromhead with the words 'You have saved not only a colony, but the credit of Old England!' Whether the fall of the post would really have led to the loss of Natal is debatable, as we have seen, but its defence certainly helped to retrieve the reputation of British arms.

For the Zulus, Rorke's Drift seems to have been regarded as best forgotten. David Rattray noted that, while the Battle of Isandlwana has featured strongly in local oral tradition up to the present day, this is not the case for the attack on the mission station.[1] The view among those who were not there seems to have been that, by crossing into Natal, Dabulamanzi and his men were disobeying the king's orders and deserved to be defeated.

Of course, memories eventually faded even in Britain, but interest in the events of 22 January revived in the 1960s, with the release of Cy Endfield and Stanley Baker's film *Zulu* in 1964, and the publication of Donald Morris's book *The Washing of the Spears* two years later. Since then a stream of books, articles, films and television documentaries has kept the subject constantly in the public eye, and the battlefield sites in what is now the KwaZulu-Natal Province of South Africa support a sizeable tourist industry. It is to be hoped that the increasing close relations between the descendants of former enemies, and the mutual respect which is encouraged by shared memories of their heroism, will be the longest-lasting legacy of the day of Isandlwana.

Notes

―――◆―――

Introduction

1. Quoted in Laband, *Lord Chelmsford's Zululand Campaign*.
2. See especially Webb & Wright, *The James Stuart Archive*.
3. Eldredge, *The Creation of the Zulu Kingdom*.
4. For the biographies of the major participants, see Greaves and Knight, *Who's Who in the Zulu War* (2 vols), and Laband, *Historical Dictionary of the Zulu Wars*.

Prologue

1. Child, *The Zulu War Journal of Colonel Henry Harford*.
2. For the origins and early history of the Zulu kingdom see Eldredge, *The Creation of the Zulu Kingdom*, Knight, *Zulu Rising*, and Laband, *Rope of Sand*.
3. *James Stuart Archive*, quoted in Spring, *African Arms and Armour*.
4. Knight, *Anatomy of the Zulu Army* (though the author seems to regard this particular tactic as a myth – see his comments on p. 102).
5. Knight, *Zulu Rising*. Laband, *Rope of Sand*.
6. Interview with Mehlokazulu in Norris Newman, *In Zululand with the British* (henceforth 'Mehlokazulu').
7. For the Zulu army see Knight, *Anatomy of the Zulu Army*.
8. Knight, *Zulu Rising*.
9. Knight, *Zulu Rising*.
10. For the Cape Frontier War of 1878, see K. Smith, *The Wedding Feast War* (London, 2012).
11. Thompson, *Black Soldiers of the Queen: The Natal Native Contingent*.
12. Crealock apparently hoped that the attack on Sihayo would also provoke Cetshwayo into 'instant action'. Quoted in Clarke, *Zululand at War*.

13. Major Clery (one of Glyn's staff) recalled that Chelmsford had ordered his artillery not to fire on the Zulus at long range, 'for fear of frightening them, and so deterring them from coming on'. Quoted in Clarke, *Zululand at War*.

14. Laband, *Kingdom in Crisis*.

15. Knight, *Zulu Rising*.

16. Penn Symons, quoted in Knight, *Zulu Rising*.

17. Child, *Zulu War Journal*.

CHAPTER 1: Before the Dawn

1. Browne, *A Lost Legionary in South Africa* (henceforth 'Browne') Child, *Zulu War Journal*, Norris-Newman, *In Zululand With the British*.

2. Clery, quoted in Clarke, *Zululand at War*.

3. Clery, quoted in Clarke, *Zululand at War*.

4. Crealock's actual order to Durnford was reproduced in Edward Durnford's biography of his brother, *A Soldier's Life and Work in South Africa* (London 1882), and has been quoted by most authors writing on the subject since.

5. Droogleever, *The Road to Isandlwana*.

6. Clery, quoted in Clarke, *Zululand at War*.

7. Nzuzi Mandla of the uVe, quoted in Knight, *Zulu Rising*.

8. Gibson, *The Story of the Zulus*.

CHAPTER 2: Early Hours

1. See Snook, *How Can Man Die Better*, for this view of the Zulu deployment. Ian Knight has eloquently contested it in his *Zulu Rising* (see his notes to Chapter 20, p. 642 of the hardback edition), but it does fit better with the timescale adopted here than the theory that the entire Zulu army had to make its way out of the Ngwebeni Valley in the few minutes after its chance discovery around 11:30.

2. Cochrane's report, quoted in Greaves, *Isandlwana*, Appendix B.

3. Chard's report to Queen Victoria, quoted in Greaves, *Rorke's Drift*, Appendix A (henceforth 'Chard').

4. Trooper Barker, quoted in Knight, *Zulu Rising*.

5. Mehlokazulu.

6. Browne.

7. Knight, *Zulu Rising*.

8. Knight, *Zulu Rising*.

9. Curling, in Greaves & Best, *The Curling Letters of the Zulu War* (henceforth 'Curling').
10. Smith-Dorrien, quoted in Knight, *Zulu Rising*.
11. Bengough, *Memories of a Soldier's Life*.
12. Bengough, *Memories of a Soldier's Life*.
13. Mehlokazulu.
14. Cochrane, quoted in Knight, *Zulu Rising*.
15. Clery, quoted in Clarke, *Zululand at War*.
16. Curling.
17. Knight, *Zulu Rising*.

CHAPTER 3: Late Morning

1. Chard.
2. Knight, *Zulu Rising*.
3. Child, *Zulu War Journal*.
4. Norris-Newman, *In Zululand with the British*.
5. Chard.
6. Colenso & Durnford, *A History of the Zulu War*.
7. Higginson's report, quoted in Knight, *Zulu Rising*. For the history, equipment and appearance of the individual Zulu regiments, see Knight, *Anatomy of the Zulu Army*.
8. Clarke, *Zululand at War*.
9. Gardner's evidence to the Court of Enquiry, quoted in Knight, *Zulu Rising*.
10. Brickhill, *Natal Magazine*, September 1879, quoted in Knight, *Zulu Rising*.
11. For the timing of this move I have followed Colonel Snook; see his note on p. 152 of *How Can Man Die Better*.
12. Browne.
13. Essex, quoted in Knight, *Zulu Rising*.
14. Browne.
15. Cochrane's report, quoted in Greaves, *Isandlwana*, Appendix B (henceforth 'Cochrane').
16. Cochrane.
17. Cochrane (note to Appendix B in Greaves, *Isandlwana*).
18. Raw's report, quoted in Knight, *Zulu Rising*.
19. Cetshwayo, quoted in Knight, *Zulu Rising*.
20. Raw's report, quoted in Knight, *Zulu Rising*.
21. Mhlahlana Ngune of the iNgobamakhosi, quoted in Knight, *Zulu Rising*.

22. For Zulu tactical doctrine, see Knight, *Anatomy of the Zulu Army*.
23. Quoted in Greaves, *Isandlwana*.
24. Curling.
25. Essex, quoted in Knight, *Zulu Rising*.
26. Chard.
27. Ndukwana kaMbengwane, *James Stuart Archive*, quoted in Knight, *Zulu Rising*.
28. Lieutenant Davies's report, quoted in Knight, *Zulu Rising*.
29. Davies's report, quoted in Knight, *Zulu Rising*.

INTERLUDE: 'Gentlemen in England now abed . . .'

1. Queen Victoria's Diary online.
2. British Newspaper Archive, January 1879.
3. For Leopold's rule in the Congo and Stanley's role in it, see A. Hochschild, *King Leopold's Ghost* (London, 1999).
4. Hochschild, *King Leopold's Ghost*.

CHAPTER 4: High Noon

1. Essex, quoted in Knight, *Zulu Rising*.
2. Stafford, quoted in Knight, *Zulu Rising*.
3. Cochrane.
4. Cochrane.
5. Nourse, quoted in Knight, *Zulu Rising*.
6. Nourse, quoted in Knight, *Zulu Rising*.
7. A. W. Lee, quoted in Knight, *Companion to the Anglo-Zulu War*.
8. Nourse, quoted in Knight, *Zulu Rising*.
9. Chard.
10. Brickhill, quoted in Knight, *Zulu Rising*.
11. Brickhill quoted in Knight, *Zulu Rising*.
12. Gardner, quoted in Knight, *Zulu Rising*.
13. Essex, quoted in Knight, *Zulu Rising*.
14. Curling.
15. Bengough, *Memories of a Soldier's Life*.
16. Cochrane.
17. Holme, *The Noble 24th*.
18. Curling.
19. Knight, *Anatomy of the Zulu Army*.

20. This at least was the version of Roberts's death reported by Lieutenant Stafford. Quoted in Greaves, *Isandlwana*.
21. Essex quoted in Knight, *Zulu Rising*.
22. Browne.
23. For reconstructions of the movements of the Undi corps at this stage of the battle, see Knight, *Zulu Rising*, p. 448, and Snook, *How Can Man Die Better*, p. 169.
24. Bourne 1936 interview, quoted in Greaves, *Rorke's Drift*, Appendix E.
25. Mehlokazulu.
26. Cochrane.
27. Essex, quoted in Knight, *Zulu Rising*.
28. Quoted in Knight, *Zulu Rising*.
29. Reynolds's report, quoted in Greaves, *Rorke's Drift*, Appendix D.
30. Quoted in Knight, *Zulu Rising*.
31. Quoted in Knight, *Zulu Rising*.
32. Pulleine's intentions at this point can only be speculation, but Colonel Snook's analysis (*How Can Man Die Better*, p. 216) seems to make good military sense.
33. Mitford, *Through the Zulu Country*. See also the note on p. 651 of Knight, *Zulu Rising*.
34. Mpashana kaSodondo, quoted in Knight, *Zulu Rising*.
35. Curling.
36. Brickhill, quoted in Knight, *Zulu Rising*.
37. We lack confirmation from Zulu sources that this was the intention, but the move is easily explained in terms of Zulu tactical doctrine, for which see Knight, *Anatomy of the Zulu Army*.
38. Pulleine's groom, Thomas Parry, quoted in Snook, *How Can Man Die Better*.
39. There has long been controversy over the question of whether Melvill was ordered to take the Colour to safety, or did so on his own initiative, possibly with the aim of facilitating his own escape. For opposing views, see Snook, *How Can Man Die Better*, p. 256, and Knight, *Zulu Rising*, p. 432.
40. Essex, quoted in Knight, *Zulu Rising*.
41. Nourse, quoted in Knight, *Zulu Rising*.
42. Durnford, *A Soldier's Life*.
43. Norris-Newman, *In Zululand with the British*.
44. H. J. P. Wilkins, *The Story of the Blood Drenched Field of Isandlwana* (Vryheid, 1939).

45. Black's report, quoted in Knight, *Zulu Rising*.
46. Browne.
47. Knight, *Zulu Rising*.
48. Essex, quoted in Knight, *Zulu Rising*.
49. Nourse, quoted in Knight, *Zulu Rising*.
50. Mehlokazulu.
51. Snook, *How Can Man Die Better*.
52. O. Watkins, quoted in Knight, *Zulu Rising*.
53. Curling.
54. Watkins, quoted in Knight, *Zulu Rising*.
55. Mehlokazulu.
56. Swinny, 'A Zulu Boy's Recollections'.
57. Brickhill, quoted in Knight, *Zulu Rising*.
58. Brickhill, quoted in Knight, *Zulu Rising*.
59. Quoted in W. H. Clements, *The Glamour and Tragedy of the Zulu War* (London 1936).
60. This anonymous account was given to the novelist H. Rider Haggard, quoted in Knight, *Zulu Rising*.
61. Nourse, quoted in Knight, *Zulu Rising*.
62. Smith-Dorrien, *Memories of Forty-Eight Years' Service*.
63. Brickhill, quoted in Knight, *Zulu Rising*.

CHAPTER 5: Afternoon

1. Browne.
2. Mehlokazulu.
3. Knight, *Anatomy of the Zulu Army*.
4. How reluctant Dabulamanzi was can only be conjectured, but according to Swinny, 'A Zulu Boy's Recollections', it was the men of the uThulwana regiment who urged him to 'go and have a fight at Jim's!'
5. Surgeon Reynolds's report, quoted in Greaves, *Rorke's Drift*, Appendix D.
6. Smith-Dorrien, *Memories of Forty-Eight Years' Service*.
7. Quoted in Knight, *Zulu Rising*.
8. Quoted in Knight, *Zulu Rising*.
9. Quoted in Knight, *Zulu Rising*.
10. Quoted in Knight, *Zulu Rising*.
11. Wassall's account, quoted in Greaves, *Isandlwana*, Appendix D.
12. Smith-Dorrien, *Memories of Forty-Eight Years' Service*.

13. Higginson's report, quoted in Knight, *Zulu Rising*. For the deaths of Melvill and Coghill, see also Colonel Glyn's report, quoted in Greaves, *Isandlwana*, Appendix C.

14. Essex, quoted in Knight, *Zulu Rising*.

15. Higginson's report, quoted in Knight, *Zulu Rising*.

16. Browne.

17. Swinny, 'A Zulu Boy's Recollections'.

18. Quoted in Knight, *Zulu Rising*.

19. Quoted in Knight, *Zulu Rising*.

20. Knight, *Zulu Rising*.

21. Russell, quoted in Knight, *Zulu Rising*.

22. Norris-Newman, *In Zululand with the British*

23. Anonymous man of the uVe regiment, quoted in Knight, *Zulu Rising*.

24. Mitford, *Through the Zulu Country*.

25. Quoted in Knight, *Zulu Rising*.

26. Stalker, *The Natal Carbineers*.

27. Spalding, quoted in Knight, *Zulu Rising*.

28. Rev. George Smith, quoted in Knight, *Zulu Rising*.

29. Chard.

30. Account of Alfred Hook in *Royal* magazine, February 1905 (henceforth 'Hook').

31. Bourne 1936, quoted in Greaves, *Rorke's Drift*.

32. Chard.

33. Reynolds, quoted in Yorke, *Rorke's Drift*.

34. Harry Lugg, quoted in Yorke, *Rorke's Drift*.

35. Chard.

36. Browne.

37. Reynolds, quoted in Yorke, *Rorke's Drift*.

CHAPTER 6: The Siege of Rorke's Drift

1. Chard.

2. Browne.

3. Colenso & Durnford, *A History of the Zulu War*.

4. Dlamini, *Servant of Two Kings*.

5. Browne.

6. Chard.

7. Hook refers to 'some of us' firing a volley which killed a 'sergeant' of the NNC, but does not name the victim. George Smith, who buried Anderson,

noted that he had been shot in the back of the head, but ascribed his death to the Zulus. See Knight, *Zulu Rising*, p. 491.

8. Chard.
9. Boucher, 'Frederick Hitch and the Defence of Rorke's Drift' (henceforth 'Hitch').
10. Browne.
11. Gosset, quoted in Major G. French, *Lord Chelmsford and the Zulu War* (London, 1939).
12. Bengough, *Memories of a Soldier's Life*.
13. Spalding, quoted in Knight, *Zulu Rising*.
14. Hitch.
15. Reynolds, quoted in Yorke, *Rorke's Drift*.
16. Howard, quoted in Yorke, *Rorke's Drift*.
17. Hook.
18. Hook.
19. Waters, quoted in Yorke, *Rorke's Drift*.
20. Attwood, quoted in Snook, *Like Wolves on the Fold*.
21. Penn Symons, quoted in Snook, *Like Wolves on the Fold*.
22. Chard.
23. Glyn's aide Capt. Henry Hallam Parr, quoted in Knight, *Zulu Rising*.
24. Quoted in Snook, *Like Wolves on the Fold*.
25. Quoted in Yorke, *Rorke's Drift*.
26. Penn Symons, quoted in Knight, *Zulu Rising*.
27. Colenso & Durnford, *A History of the Zulu War*.
28. Hook.
29. Chard.
30. Rev. Smith, quoted in Yorke.
31. Rev. Smith, quoted in Knight, *Zulu Rising*.
32. Chard.
33. Dlamini, *Servant of Two Kings*.
34. Chard.
35. Chard.
36. Waters, quoted in Yorke, *Rorke's Drift*.
37. Trooper Symons, quoted in Knight, *Zulu Rising*.
38. Essex, quoted in Knight, *Zulu Rising*.
39. Hook.
40. Browne.

41. Dunne, quoted in Yorke, *Rorke's Drift*.
42. Hook.
43. Chard.
44. Hook.
45. Chard.
46. Several eyewitnesses described what Harford called the 'ghastly sight' of the battlefield. See Knight, *Zulu Rising*, pp. 465–8.
47. Browne.
48. Hitch.
49. Hitch.
50. Chard.
51. Hitch.
52. Chard.

CHAPTER 7: The Night Battle

1. Browne.
2. Spalding, quoted in Knight, *Zulu Rising*.
3. Reynolds's report, quoted in Greaves, *Rorke's Drift*, Appendix D.
4. Chard.
5. Spalding, quoted in Knight, *Zulu Rising*.
6. Chard.
7. Dunne, quoted in Yorke, *Rorke's Drift*.
8. Chard.
9. Lugg, quoted in Yorke, *Rorke's Drift*.
10. Hook.
11. Spalding, quoted in Knight, *Zulu Rising*.

CHAPTER 8: 23 January

1. Hallam Parr, quoted in Yorke, *Rorke's Drift*.
2. Browne.
3. Chard.
4. Chard.
5. Child, *Zulu War Journal*.
6. Swinny, 'A Zulu Boy's Recollections'.
7. Lieutenant J. Maxwell, quoted in Knight, *Zulu Rising*.
8. Chard.
9. Child, *Zulu War Journal*.

10. Dunne, quoted in Knight, *Zulu Rising*.
11. Hook.
12. Chard.

CHAPTER 9: Aftermath

1. For subsequent events in Zululand, see especially Laband (ed.), *Lord Chelmsford's Zululand Campaign*, and Guy, *The Destruction of the Zulu Kingdom*.
2. For the later careers of the surviving participants, see Greaves and Knight, *Who's Who in the Zulu War*, Laband, *Historical Dictionary of the Zulu Wars*, and Greaves, *Rorke's Drift* and *Isandlwana*.
3. For the controversy over Chelmsford's responsibility for the disaster at Isandlwana, see especially Greaves, *Isandlwana*.
4. Knight, *Zulu Rising*.
5. Captain W. Jones, quoted in Knight, *Zulu Rising*.
6. Yorke, *Rorke's Drift*.
7. The transcript is reproduced as Appendix E in Greaves, *Rorke's Drift*.

Conclusion

1. Rattray, *The Day of the Dead Moon* (audio book).

Sources and Suggested Reading

There have been countless books and articles published on the Anglo-Zulu War and the events of 22 January in particular. I am grateful for the assistance of John Laband in pointing me towards many of these sources, although of course he is not responsible for any of my errors or omissions.

Books and Articles

Beckett, Ian, F. W. *Battles in Focus: Isandlwana 1879* (London: Brassey's, 2003)
——, *Rorke's Drift and Isandlwana* (Oxford: Oxford University Press, 2019)
Bengough, H. M., *Memories of a Soldier's Life* (London: Edward Arnold, 1913)
Boucher, M., 'Frederick Hitch and the Defence of Rorke's Drift', *Military History Journal*, South African Military History Society, Vol. 2, No. 6, 1973

Child, Daphne (ed.), *The Zulu War Journal of Colonel Henry Harford, C.B.* (Pietermaritzburg: Shuter & Shooter, 1978)
Clarke, Sonia, *Invasion of Zululand 1879: Anglo-Zulu War Experiences of Arthur Harness; John Jervis, 4th Viscount St Vincent; and Sir Henry Bulwer* (Houghton: Brenthurst Press, 1979)
——, *Zululand at War: The Conduct of the Anglo-Zulu War* (Houghton: Brenthurst Press, 1984)
Colenso, F. E., assisted by Durnford, Lt.-Col. E., *A History of the Zulu War and its Origin* (London: 1880)

Dlamini, Paulina, *Servant of Two Kings*, compiled by H. Filter and edited and translated by S. Bourquin (Durban: Killie Campbell Africana Library; Pieter-maritzburg: University of Natal Press, 1986)

Droogleever, R. W. F., *The Road to Isandhlwana: Colonel Anthony Durnford in Natal and Zululand* (London: Greenhill, 1992)

Eldredge, Elizabeth, *The Creation of the Zulu Kingdom, 1815–1828* (Cambridge University Press, 2014)

Gibson, J. Y., *The Story of the Zulus* (London: Longman, Green, 1911)
Gon, Philip, *The Road to Isandlwana: The Years of an Imperial Battalion* (Johannesburg: Ad. Donker, 1979)
Greaves, Adrian, *Rorke's Drift* (London: Cassell, 2002)
—, *Isandlwana: How the Zulus Humbled the British Empire* (Barnsley: Pen & Sword Military, 2011)
Greaves, Adrian and Brian Best (eds), *The Curling Letters of the Zulu War. 'There Was Awful Slaughter'* (Barnsley: Leo Cooper, 2001)
Greaves, Adrian and Ian Knight, *Who's Who in the Zulu War*, Vol. I: *The British*; Vol. II: *Colonials and Zulus* (Barnsley: Pen & Sword Military, 2006 & 2007)
Guy, J., *The Destruction of the Zulu Kingdom: The Civil War in Zululand* (Pieter-maritzburg, University of Natal Press, 1994)

Hamilton-Browne, Col. G. A., *Lost Legionary in South Africa* (London: T. Werner Laurie, 1912)
Holme, N., *The Silver Wreath: Being the 24th Regiment at Isandhlwana and Rorke's Drift* (London: 1979)
—, *The Noble 24th* (London: Savannah Publications, 1999)

Knight, Ian, *Nothing Remains but to Fight: The Defence of Rorke's Drift, 1879* (London: Greenhill Books, 1993)
—, *Rorke's Drift 1879: 'Pinned Like Rats in a Hole'* (Oxford: Osprey Military Campaign Series 41, 1996)
—, *Isandlwana 1879: 'The Great Zulu Victory'* (Oxford: Osprey Military Campaign Series 111, 2002)
—, *Companion to the Anglo Zulu War* (Barnsley: Pen & Sword, 2008)
—, *Zulu Rising: The Epic Story of Isandlwana and Rorke's Drift* (London: Macmillan, 2010. The original hardback edition contains comprehensive notes and references, but these are not in the paperback edition published in 2011, though they can be accessed online.)
—, *The Anatomy of the Zulu Army* (Barnsley, Frontline Books, revised edition, 2015)

Laband, John, *Fight Us in the Open: The Anglo-Zulu War through Zulu Eyes* (Pietermaritzburg: Shuter & Shooter; Ulundi: KwaZulu Monuments Council, 1985)

—— (ed.), *Lord Chelmsford's Zululand Campaign 1878–1879* (Stroud: Alan Sutton Publishing for the Army Records Society, 1994)

——, *Rope of Sand: The Rise and Fall of the Zulu kingdom in the Nineteenth Century* (Johannesburg: Jonathan Ball, 1995)

——, *Kingdom in Crisis: the Zulu Response to the British Invasion of 1879* (Barnsley: Pen & Sword, 2007)

——, *Historical Dictionary of the Zulu Wars* (Lanham: Scarecrow Press, 2009)

——, 'Zulu Wars', in Dennis Showalter (ed.), *Oxford Bibliographies Online: Military History* (New York: Oxford University Press, 2012)

——, *Zulu Warriors: The Battle for the South African Frontier* (New Haven and London: Yale University Press, 2014)

——, *The Fall of Rorke's Drift: An Alternate History of the Anglo Zulu War of 1879* (Barnsley: Greenhill Books, 2019)

Laband, John and Ian Knight, *The War Correspondents: The Anglo-Zulu War* (Stroud: Sutton Publishing, 1996)

Laband, John (series editor) and Knight, Ian (volume editor), *Archives of Zululand* Vol. 4: *The Anglo-Zulu War 1879* (London: Archival Publications International, 2000)

Laband, John, and Paul Thompson, *The Illustrated Guide to the Anglo-Zulu War* (Pietermaritzburg: University of Natal Press, 2000)

Lock, R. and P. Quantrill, *Zulu Victory: The Epic of Isandlwana and the Cover-up* (London: Greenhill Books, 2002)

Manning, Stephen, *The Martini-Henry Rifle* (Oxford: Osprey Weapon Series 26; 2013

Mitford, Bertram, *Through the Zulu Country: Its Battlefields and Its People* (London: Kegan, Paul, Trench, 1883)

Morris, Donald R., *The Washing of the Spears* (London: Jonathan Cape, 1966)

Norris-Newman, Charles, *In Zululand with the British* (London: W. H. Allen, 1880)

Peers, Chris, *Rorke's Drift & Isandlwana, A Battlefield Guide* (Stroud: History Press, 2017)

Pegler, Martin, *Powder and Ball Small Arms* (Marlborough: Crowood Press, 1998)

Smith-Dorrien, General Sir H., *Memories of Forty-Eight Years' Service* (London: John Murray, 1925)

Snook, Lt.-Col. Mike, *Like Wolves on the Fold: The Defence of Rorke's Drift* (Barnsley: Frontline Books, revised edition, 2010)

——, *How Can Man Die Better: The Secrets of Isandlwana Revealed* (Barnsley: Frontline Books, revised edition, 2018)

Spring, C., *African Arms and Armour* (London: British Museum Press, 1993)

Stalker, J., *The Natal Carbineers* (Pietermaritzburg, 1912)

Swinny, G. H., 'A Zulu Boy's Recollections of the Zulu War', ed. C. de B. Webb, *Natalia* 8, December 1878, pp. 8–21

Thompson, Paul, *Black Soldiers of the Queen: The Natal Native Contingent in the Anglo-Zulu War* (Tuscaloosa: University of Alabama Press, 2006)

Vijn, Cornelius, *Cetshwayo's Dutchman: Being the Private Journal of a White Trader in Zululand during the British Invasion*, ed. Bishop J. W. Colenso (London: Longmans, Green, 1880)

War Office, Intelligence Division, *Narrative of the Field Operations Connected with the Zulu War of 1879* (London: Her Majesty's Stationery Office, 1881)

Webb, Colin de B. and John Wright (eds), *The James Stuart Archive of Recorded Oral Evidence Relating to the History of the Zulu and Neighbouring Peoples*, 6 vols (Pietermaritzburg: University of Natal Press; Durban: Killie Campbell Africana Library, 1976, 1979, 1982, 1986, 2001, 2014 [JSA])

—— (eds), *A Zulu King Speaks: Statements Made by Cetshwayo kaMpande on the History and Customs of His People* (Pietermaritzburg: University of Natal Press; Durban: Killie Campbell Africana Library, 1978)

Yorke, Edmund, *Rorke's Drift 1879: Anatomy of an Epic Zulu War Siege* (Stroud: Tempus, 2001)

Online Sources

The British Newspaper Archive, at www.britishnewspaperarchive.co.uk

Queen Victoria's Journals, at www.queenvictoriasjournals.org

Audio

Also highly recommended is David Rattray's audio book, 'The Day of the Dead Moon', which is available as a set of CDs or an MP3 download from the Anglo Zulu War Historical Society at info@anglozuluwar.com. The late David Rattray of Fugitives' Drift Lodge was a well-known local historian and tour guide who did a great deal to popularise the battlefields and the events which took place there, before his tragic death in 2007.

Index